LEADERSHIP RESILIENCE IN A DIGITAL AGE

The book focusses on the challenges faced in the digital age, and the increasing demands for continuous change in an inter-connected digital world. The book presents stories about how leaders have faced significant challenges and pressure, and how they have used these experiences as catalysts to transform, flourish, and develop personal resilience. The book explores the digital journey, ethical issues, teamwork, styles of leadership, agile, collaboration, trust, culture, psychological safety, self-awareness, vulnerability, conversation, positivity, emotional intelligence, creativity, inner knowing and the dark side of leadership.

Drawing on the experiences of leaders in the creative, digital and technology sectors in the UK, and using their voice throughout, has resulted in proposing several internal and external strategic solutions to help the reader become more personally resilient. The book explores the impact of continuous change within a digital age, presenting the facets necessary to become a Digital Sage in an increasingly chaotic world. With a focus on creativity, innovation and mind and body awareness the leader as a Digital Sage arises to encourage resilience in a digital age.

The book does not assume prior knowledge of the field of resilience and is ideal for executive education courses, and for leaders and managers seeking personal and professional transformation.

Janette Young is an experienced senior academic, consultant and coach, most recently director of a suite of MSC e-business programmes at the Newcastle University Business School and author of *Personal Knowledge Capital: The Inner and Outer Path of Knowledge Creation in a Web World.*

LEADERSHIP RESILIENCE IN A DIGITAL AGE

Janette Young, PhD

Routledge
Taylor & Francis Group
LONDON AND NEW YORK

First published 2022
by Routledge
2 Park Square, Milton Park, Abingdon, Oxon OX14 4RN

and by Routledge
605 Third Avenue, New York, NY 10158

Routledge is an imprint of the Taylor & Francis Group, an informa business

British Library Cataloguing-in-Publication Data
A catalogue record for this book is available from the British Library

Library of Congress Cataloging-in-Publication Data
A catalog record for this book has been requested

ISBN: 978-0-367-28096-3 (hbk)
ISBN: 978-1-032-04774-4 (pbk)
ISBN: 978-0-367-28097-0 (ebk)

DOI: 10.4324/9780367280970

Typeset in Joanna
by Apex CoVantage, LLC

This book is dedicated to Diane Young for her support and review of the draft book.

I would like to dedicate my thanks to my commissioning editor Rebecca Marsh, Senior Editor at Taylor & Francis for having faith in me.

Finally, gratitude and thanks go to all of the leaders in the creative digital community of the North of England who contributed their time to enable the research interviews to take place. All the names have been anonymised. It was a privilege to listen to your stories.

CONTENTS

FIGURES

PREFACE

Introduction

Throughout this book I focus on contemporary leadership and argue that digital leaders not only require strategic thinking and excellent communication skills, but they also need to show a strong ethical compass, authenticity, compassion, kindness, empathy, creativity, knowingness, flexibility and entrepreneurship. They need mechanisms for fast and decisive decision-making along with perseverance, tenacity and resilience that enables them to have the ability to navigate within the new norm, which is a physical, mental and virtual ecology within the workplace. Additionally, the contemporary leader needs to be tech savvy and have a strategic awareness of the acceleration to digital. Today's leaders need to be endowed with an abundance of increasingly soft skills to add to their portfolio. The book is written from a "big picture" perspective and, as such, scans across an array of theoretical underpinnings, whilst blending this with the quotes and stories from the qualitative research. A main goal has been to explore and highlight individual personal resilience and discover the strategies that as leaders we may all need to take into consideration in order to survive in the future.

My motivation for writing the book and undertaking the underpinning research and design derives from a belief that more needs to be explored in the area of resilience within our increasingly fast moving digital environment. Whilst originally writing my first book published in 2012, *Personal Knowledge Capital: the inner and outer path of knowledge creation in a web world*, the seed began to emerge that I needed to write another book this time on leadership. The questions were focused around: How do we survive in this increasingly complex and digital and knowledge focused world? Since then, the ideas for this book have been brewing and came to fruition after the empirical research took place. The book has been informed by data from the leadership interviews. I believe the comments and stories bring the book to life and add credibility to the messages put forward. The research quotes and stories presented arise from a qualitative inductive study made up of 25 interviewees from leaders in the creative, digital sector of the North East of England collected in 2018 and 2019. The interviews took place in person either at the interviewees place of work or at the University. The names of the individual leaders have been anonymised for the sake of confidentiality. The data was transcribed and analysed using software and you will find stories and quotes from the data used to underpin each chapter in the book. Additionally, this resulted in the presentation of an array of tools and frameworks for personal resilience.

Every leader is undoubtedly on a journey and many features will need to be explored on the path. Therefore, this book seeks to explore what personal resilience looks like when embracing the innovative, creative, dynamic, complex, changing, environments where new business models have been informed by the constant impact of technology. The outcome from the book takes an internal and external perspective that captures a mind, body and wellbeing approach to contemporary leadership. The conclusions from the research offer an array of preventative strategies and solutions to develop personal resilience and capture the essence of an array of facets for leaders for what turned into the Digital Sage.

1

THE JOURNEY

The new order

We are stepping into a new world order and digital age. In a climate of increasing complexity and uncertainty, there are global issues to contend with including dwindling resources, natural catastrophes across the globe and climate change (possibly the highest priority that has to be addressed). Pandemics have also arrived to create havoc and fear. Moreover, new technologies bring a blistering pace of change, including the introduction of artificial intelligence and augmented reality. As if this is not enough for humanity to cope with, the new technologies have resulted in changing business models and accelerated trends that impact business at break-neck speed. Today, we need to learn from the lessons of the past and focus on long-term strategies for man's future evolution for a regenerative and restorative economy where business leaders collaborate to forge a new, harmonious, positive future where initiatives for a regenerative climate change and the natural world are built into the values of the company. We cannot escape the fact that we all too often act in short-sighted

DOI: 10.4324/9780367280970-1

self-interest and have difficulty perceiving the greater good as more important than our personal interests (Dobie & Koeplin 2020). As such, we need to be aware of the new paradigms where power and influence change hands.

This world and the business landscape that we operate in are increasingly uncertain and volatile. Decisions are made at break-neck speed; we are increasingly operating within a VUCA (volatile, uncertain, complex and ambiguous) landscape. VUCA was an acronym originally used by the American military to describe extreme conditions. Military leaders coined the term in the early 1990's to describe the destabilized world conditions precipitated by the fall of communism and the end of the cold war, and today it is used to express the supposedly unique environment facing leaders (Spector 2019). How then do managers and leaders respond to an ever changing and complex environment? How do they prepare for the pace of change in a digital environment? What styles of leadership do we have to develop to survive and de-risk in the future? Leaders have to contend with the onslaught of a blistering pace of change and ever-changing technologies and automation that are creating a complex environment in which to operate. In the new digital world, speed and agility are of the essence.

The backdrop to this complex context, is to consider complexity theory. A way of understanding the difficulties that may be encountered. Complexity leadership theory (CLT) is about balancing formal and informal organization to leverage the dynamics of complex adaptive systems (CAS) and produce learning, creativity, and adaptation in organisations (Bäcklander 2019). The nature of knowledge-oriented organisations and their environments seems to dictate the increased use of networked, collective ways of working where the sum of interactions is greater than the individual parts – called adaptive space in complex leadership theory (Bäcklander 2019). Viewing the environment from the lens of complexity theory helps us to understand the context in which leaders find themselves within management today. By doing so, scholars have begun to embrace complexity within leadership and have begun to explore this concept, albeit tentatively, to try to understand the impact of the rapidly changing business environment.

Managing the change

In management, the theories based on the old static order do not survive anymore. As mentioned above, we are now enveloped in an era of constant change that is spearheaded by the impact of constantly updated technologies. We can no longer look at management theory by using models and tools designed for a traditional and static environment of yesteryear. Today's leaders will be aware of the impact of change on themselves and staff. The current inter-connected digital i-environment we live in can be viewed as organic and, as such, we must adapt and adjust to the constant change. In the past management was viewed through a static linear lens. This is no longer the case and managers and leaders need to regularly review the impact of change in an evolving, complex and networked i-connected world. We need to view management through a new lens created for a less linear more dynamic environment. How then do leaders ride the tide of change and prepare for the future of work and the impact that these unforeseeable changes have on business and individuals?

As part of the technology evolution, we all participate in stepping outside our comfort zones on a regular basis. The comfort zone is a place where you feel safe and in control, whilst the fear zone shows a lack of self-confidence and is a place where you may be easily affected by other opinions. Extending into a learning zone means that we begin to deal with new challenges and problems. In the learning zone you acquire new skills and extend your comfort zone. In the growth zone you begin to live your purpose, live your dreams, learn and set new goals and conquer objectives. However, if the stretch becomes "stress" then burnout is possible and wellbeing is at risk, as excessive challenges can induce destructive stress. It is important for leaders to appreciate comfort verses stretch and become aware when the stretch expands too far for comfort. Understanding and being aware of the processes involved in managing this change is helpful. Whilst leaders and employers need stretch, they don't want burnout and it is employing a balance, that can sustain the organisation.

From a theoretical point of view, the Kubler-Ross (1969) five-stage change cycle model can be used to track the leader's journey through any significant change. The model highlights that until everyone has reached acceptance of the new initiative, the job is not done. Originally, the Kubler-Ross five-stage grief cycle was intended to help people deal with bereavement, however, it was quickly adapted to reflect the stages of any change event in the professional management sector. The five stages of the model include a first stage of denial: which is an initial stage of numbness and sense of disbelief. As such there may be a refusal to accept the imminent change. The second stage is anger: when acceptance of the reality of the situation occurs. At this stage denial turns to anger. The third stage is bargaining: this is intended to resolve the problem faced or put off the inevitable. The next stage is depression: this stage is reached when bargaining fails, and the reality of the situation sets in and as such loss is felt. The final stage five is acceptance: this involves dealing with regret and is a necessary pre-requisite for acceptance. Acceptance is reached when the individual realises that change is permanent. Despite the various stages, Kubler-Ross highlight that individuals don't move around this in a well-ordered sequential manner, rather they may experience various stages. An understanding of these processes is especially important in a VUCA (volatile, unpredictable, complex, ambiguous) environment where change is happening at rapid speed. Individuals are thus exposed to this cycle of change on a regular basis and as such may need extra support.

John Kotter's eight-step change approach applies big picture thinking to change management that helps the leader/manager to communicate more effectively to maximise a change project. Kotter's (1996, 2012) original eight-step process of change involves the following: establish a sense of urgency; form essential coalitions; develop a vision for the change; communicate the vision; remove obstacles; generate short-term wins; build on wins; embed changes into the organisation's culture. Communicating the change involves communicate, communicate, communicate multiplied by 10 and then 100. In other words when change arises make sure you have communicated what will occur many times over. The Kubler-Ross change cycle and the Kotter stages both help to guide us through the process and reactions that we might encounter as we pass through phases of change. Resilient leaders evolve so that they can ride the waves of change and as such one element may involve incorporating the Kubler-Ross change cycle to help understand the reactions of those around you to major change initiatives. Whilst the above discussion focuses on traditional change management models that are required for management and this may be useful, the real question is how do we respond within the context of continuous, complex rapid change? In the future new models will be needed to feature, address and respond to the continuous climate of change that we are currently witnessing.

Looking to the future

Futurists have a role to play in helping us understand some of these issues. One response is from futurist Cheesewright (2020) who from an organisational perspective talks about responding by creating a change of philosophy. He discusses three different ways to adapt to the new shifts taking place. The first about how we sense the future. This involves looking at what might happen in both the current and near future in the business. He suggests looking at the macro trends in the market and how they might collide with your business (for instance big data, artificial intelligence, augmented reality and the internet of things (IOT). He encourages going out and talking to people and peers for a deep dive into the organisation. In this way, he proposes leaders should scan the horizon every six months and keep these time-scales short. His second point is that companies need fast, accelerated decision-making responses. Cheesewright believes that currently information can move too slowly through organisations and that organisations need to push power to the edge of organisation and give out more autonomy to encourage more responsiveness. Small company founders need to think about how they can release and let go of control and be willing to share power. This may involve a change of behaviour, even when behaviour involves cultural change from those who are invested and embedded in the system and are reluctant to change. Cheesewright argues that in this age of sweeping change, we need adaptability. He argues that you can be great at what you do and still fail, if what you do is not what the customer wants any more. He is of the opinion that the recipe for sustainable success in this age of high frequency change is all about adaptability. His third point involves the shape and structure of the organisation. Cheesewright believes organisations have become too monolithic and centralised and that they need to become smart organisations that are agile and adaptable. Creating an age of adaption not optimisation! As such, an organisation needs to work in functional units, where the units are given greater autonomy and flexibility. Moreover, he argues that you need to streamline your organisation so that it is agile enough to adapt to change, which may involve building a new culture.

Consolidating the above elements helps create new responses required of digital leaders in a fast-paced digital era. This has resulted in Figure 1.1 which highlights the context, the response and resilience aspects in organisations that leaders need to consider in the future.

Attributes of leaders

A contemporary focus on the attributes of leaders from a change, complexity and leadership perspective have been put forward by O'Neill and

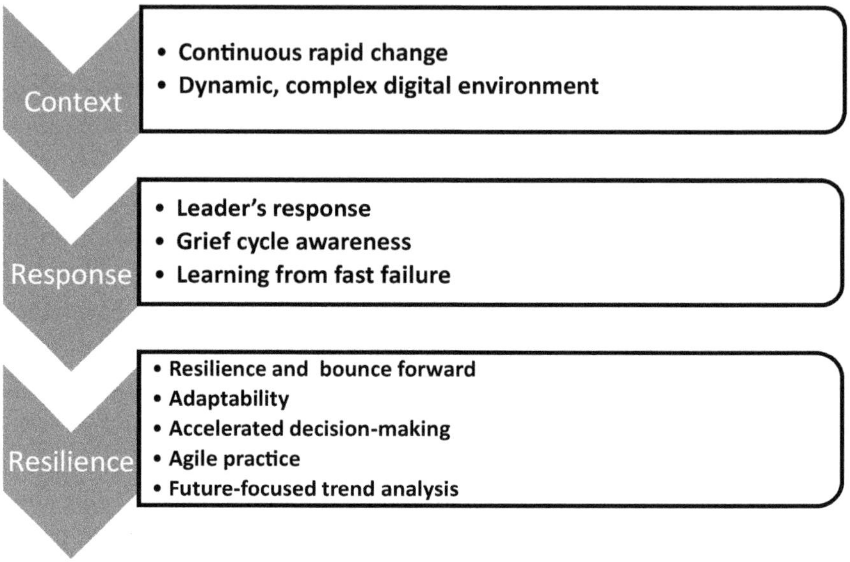

Figure 1.1 Context and responses for resilience in a rapidly changing digital era (Young, 2018–2019)

Nalbandian's (2018) empirical qualitative research within the public sector. They proposed nine leadership attributes that are required for successful leadership in the complex and highly diffused power structure of local government. They emphasise that no one person would likely possess strengths in all the attributes but believe that it is important to try to develop a leadership team with complementary strengths covering all of them. The nine attributes include: developing design literacy in all leaders; architecture for success; working small to achieve large vision; confronting the brutal facts but staying focused and consistent; creating space for innovation; the power of questions; being decisive; connecting the power of story; and symphonic skills. They emphasise that team leadership as an evolving concept is revealed in the number of metaphors, they have used to describe the profile including for example symphonic, design literacy and architecture of success. The symphonic emphasis is a nod to leading an orchestra with many different instruments and artists who each bring their own talent and skill about how a piece should be played. They argue that behind the scenes rehearsals invoke trial and error and experimentation, which are part of current design thinking. In this respect, they affirm the leader as an artist by nature. In their second observation they stress that leadership puts a premium on personal qualities and a predisposition to self-awareness. This is very likely to draw on personal talents, skills and cognitive maps as guides to action. As such, they propose that in the public sector the overriding leadership quality in the dynamic local government environment is self-awareness. However, one can argue that these are also attributes necessary for the private sector and not just the public sector in a digital business environment.

I am on a journey

Consider the metaphor of the tree. The tree has roots in the ground that allow it to dig deep. It grows new branches, and it sways in the wind but with its strong central core it goes back to its central position when the winds die down. With the different seasons of the year there are different winds of change, but the tree's deep roots allow it to sway in the wind and still go back to core. We are all impacted by environmental factors in the same ways. For leaders, this could be led by external forces – disruptive change headed by constantly changing technologies. Leaders are on a journey of discovery. They need to understand themselves and both the distractors and attractors of leadership styles. In other words, leaders are Journeyers on a journey of self-discovery, learning and improving along the way as they tap into their inner strength, to ride the tides of change and establish the evolution of new ways of working. Learning and reflecting are a major part of the journey for the leader. The ability to fast fail, learn from failure and reflect on their context is very much part of this. Schon (1984) talks about reflection in terms of reflecting IN and reflecting ON. Reflection can be in the moment (IN); or it can be after the event (ON), as such the ability to continuously reflect and learn is a key management skill. Additionally, reflexive abilities ensure that you can reflect on your own in-built assumptions. In this way, as you change the lens through which you look, you may see your own limiting perspective. Thus, reflective practice can lead to transformational change.

The journey from manager to leader

Stepping up and taking up a new position that involves leadership whether that be in a team or leading the company means that the old skill set many not suffice. Whilst many business and management schools are still teaching business models suitable for a static approach to management, these approaches may not be adaptable to the new context, where hybrid working in virtual ecologies is the new norm. Added to this, is the need to appreciate that managers may focus on the detail (the design and control of work) whilst the leader is required to create a vision of the future to set a direction and generate the energy to change, which becomes part of the organisational strategy. One key aspect to big picture thinking is to create a vision and pathway on a roadmap that acknowledges future trends. In addition is the ability to communicate this with meaningful storytelling. Another main aspect is to build trusting relationships among the teams and the wider organisation. Building teams also requires a balanced skill set of hard and soft skills, however, what will be necessary in a virtual ecology will be the technical skill acquired and the need to develop and apply social and emotional intelligence online when communicating. It is the role of the leader to use their soft skills to inspire and develop staff. Moreover, in this volatile environment decisive decision-making at speed is required.

In the following quote a digital director discusses the challenges of making the right decisions, developing and maintaining relations and setting a culture of intuition to find the energy when transforming from manager to leader.

> *"You know, one of the challenges of going from management to leadership is that in management mode you judge others and yourself not by the intensity of your industry but the quantity and quality of that, right. Leadership is less about presenteeism and is more about making the right decisions and developing and maintaining relationships with people and setting the culture of intuition to find the energy and all of that stuff that we talked about and you know when you're used to the management mode it is kind of a scary place to go."*
>
> Male Managing Director of a digital company

Good leadership and poor leadership

The interviewee data suggested that good leaders were supportive, motivating, inspiring, fair and emotionally intelligent. As one leader acknowledges in the interview, "I think with great leaders it is not what they do it's how they make you feel" (male International Coach and Consultant). All the interview respondents discussed how when looking back their good leaders were motivating and supportive. Many leaders questioned replied that they did not stay in organisations long where they identified poor leadership styles. Some of the themes arising are discussed next.

Freedom and valuing talent

This female creative digital leader discusses her previous positive experience at a company which valued her talent.

> *"I don't like unnecessary rules, and I like having flexibility. Just having that flex – I loved that. Making decisions about the business. Let's take the teams to New York! It is all very exciting – being part of the decision-making. Yes, I like that. It was nice to be at the top end of that. It opened-up that opportunity massively. To be able to have that free-reign was great."*
>
> Female Serial Entrepreneur

Sadly, many leaders never step out of the managerial role, even when they step up to become leaders. Leadership is not easily defined or measured. Very often there is inadequate training.

Incompetent leaders

Poor leaders can be incompetent leaders! They don't know how bad they really are. Many do not know the baseline of good leadership and many are still trapped in the world of traditional, command and control and transactional leadership from yesteryear. Many have not crossed over to become visionary or strategic leaders who know how to let go and delegate. Poor leaders cross the boundaries of confidentiality and trust and, in so doing, as they violate boundaries, they abuse their position of power. These leaders use their power to manipulate others because they can. The question is how do we work with people who are trustworthy in the long-term? From the interviews it became apparent that many had experienced poor leadership, and this helped them realise that they no longer wanted to work for other people once they had become highly motivated to set up their own businesses. This was a particular theme running throughout the data. "The meanness of the manager" box provides an example where a female entrepreneur discusses her past managerial experiences.

THE MEANNESS OF THE MANAGER

This environment taught me how not to manage and what not to do, now I am an employer. Looking back at one company where I worked – in the past – oh the way they managed staff! There wasn't a day someone wasn't crying. They were mean and wanted blood out of you really. You didn't feel valued at all. You just felt beaten down.

I felt pressured by my family to stay there, but after three years I had a melt down and decided not to go back.

My first experience of management was the worst and really took a toll on how I progressed, how I presented myself; how I felt about going for different job opportunities, or how I felt about myself, or how I went about going to work. That was really difficult to overcome.

Female Serial Entrepreneur

The female entrepreneur's story above highlights the early year experiences that led to a melt-down, followed by positive experiences working with a visionary leader who inspired her, and lead her to reflect upon the journey before making new decisions that cumulated in becoming a successful entrepreneur in her own right. The experience of working in different environments and cultures, with different leaders, was enlightening and led to her never looking back.

This next interviewee is emphasising the jump that many managers must take from managing to leading. There is no doubt that many leaders struggle with moving to the next level, encountering loneliness, isolation and lack of preparedness.

This example is from a creative digital leader on identifying poor leadership.

Poor leadership style

"He was quite aloof, there were times where he was quite rude to the team. There was one occasion where he insulted a couple of the team members by the way he treated them in a meeting, and, to be quite honest, the way that I saw it was that he was rude to them because he was covering his own shortcomings. Like basically he was trying to claim that he put them in a situation that he knew about and apparently afterwards, once he knew he was in the wrong he refused to apologise – 'why should I?', showing the opposites of someone who should be showing humility, and I just thought that was really poor."

"And the guy that they bought in, he's an interesting one, I mean I wouldn't have quite rated him for that role anyway, and then he came in and basically said, 'oh this is the way I'm going to do it,' and those who disagreed with him, he just got rid of and he's basically got pretty much a new board together. With a couple of exceptions, he got rid of people from the staff and I just think, again, it's to disguise his shortcomings. He was being a little bit ruthless but also I think he was just protecting himself. The qualities that he was showing were really bad, but he was protecting himself at the cost of the organisation. Whereas the previous incumbent would protect the organisation even if it meant that they would put themselves in the firing line, quite the opposite."

Male Chief Executive of creative business

Another interviewee quoted the following, highlighting the possibility of manipulation and manufactured charisma.

Leadership manipulation and crossing boundaries

"There's bad leadership, which is leadership where people understand how to manipulate other people. So, actually, it comes across as being genuine but what they're doing behind the scenes is just they are asking people to break the law. The word betray is a strong word but, actually, what they're doing is they're crossing boundaries. They're violating boundaries in terms of confidentiality and trust and what they're doing is they're using their position of power to manipulate people to do things or to suck things up and accept things that they don't have to do. So, I think that organisations are like that, human beings are like that and it's like how do we work with people who are actually trustworthy in the long term."

Male Creative Digital Founder

Manager to leader incompetence

"So, there are people who are managers, who aspire to be leaders but, actually, they're incompetent in terms of leadership because they think they're a leader, but they've been coached into it, but they don't have it within them; there's no 'there' there. They don't

> *actually know how to be a leader, how to embody that. And they stay being a manager because that's what they know, okay? So, that's just incompetent leadership."*
>
> Male Creative Digital Founder

> *"And there are too many examples of corporate organisations, religious and other leaders who are basically . . . they're acting out a role and its win/lose. So, they win and other people lose because, what they do is just manipulate other people to get their own way."*
>
> Male Leader

The above discussion and quotes highlight the need to appreciate what good leadership looks like. Olsen (2014) suggests that we should remember that any successful political leader, artist, scientist or Olympic athlete has had many failures. What separates the leaders from the losers is that they learn from their difficulties, make adjustments, and go on. Like bamboo, they bend, but do not break. Persevering, they stay the course to reach the finish line. This is a philosophy for successful leaders where learning and progressing are part of the journey.

Summary

The leader who works both individually and collaboratively with colleagues is a person on a journey who sees himself as being a Journeyer, learning from the experiences encountered. The journey can be arduous, hazardous and/or exciting and harmonious, depending on the circumstances, but often it is both. The vision should be clear but the experience and learning acquired on the way supports the leader's journey of discovery. The new normal is constant change and understanding the context and finding the determination to survive under these conditions is important. Managers are often promoted above their abilities and not all succeed in making the jump to being an effective leader. As this research data confirms, there is an awareness that some managers get stuck at the managerial level and this makes them less than competent leaders and oft times destructive individuals. However, good leaders view themselves as Journeyers who learn to respond to changing contexts that are unique to their business and circumstances. They have determination, adaptability, an ability to make accelerated decision-making and use design and agile practice for resilience, thereby adjusting to the setbacks at speed as they learn that this journey is unique to themselves.

The Journeyer (meaning men and women) embrace becoming an artist and orchestrator of the team, adapting to constant change, learning from fast failure and taking an ever evolving attitude to self-discovery and being collaborative. The Journeyer has an adaptive nature and is an agile learner.

References

Bäcklander G (2019) Doing Complexity Leadership Theory: How Agile Coaches at Spotify Practise Enabling Leadership, *Creativity and Innovation Management*, 28:1, 42–60

Cheesewright T (2020) *Future-Proof Your Business*, Penguin Business, London

Dobie D & Koeplin T (2020) *Creative Company: How Artful Creation Helps Organizations to Surpass Themselves* https://ageofartists.org Access November 2020

Kotter J P (1996, 2012) *Leading Change*, Harvard Business Review Press, Boston, MA

Kubler-Ross E (1969) *On Death and Dying*, Touchstone, New York

Olsen P E (2014) Namaste: How Yoga Can Inform Leadership Education, *Journal of Leadership Education*, 13, 116

O'Neill R J & Nalbandian J (2018) Change, Complexity, and Leadership Challenges, *Public Administration Review*, 78:2, 311–314

Schon D A (1984) *The Reflective Practitioner: How Professionals Think in Action*, Basic Books, New York

Spector B A (2019) *Discourse of Leadership: A Critical Appraisal*, Cambridge University Press, New York

Young J (2018–2019) *Research Interview Insights on Resilience Study*, The Creative Digital Community, North East, UK. Research first published in this volume

2

THE DIGITAL AGE

Change, Culture and Ethics

The winds of change have arrived! Prepare windmills

Prepare to create windmills! Today we are at the beginning of a fourth Industrial Revolution. Developments in the tech field such as mobile internet, cloud technologies, internet of things, artificial intelligence, augmented reality, advanced robotics, nanotechnology, 3D printing, genetics and biotechnology are being amplified in industry. The transition to digital ways of working has been accelerated by the 2020 global pandemic. This experience has led to a major paradigm shift across the globe, resulting in the usage of virtual tools. The wind was blowing with extreme gusto in 2020! All organisations need to create windmills for survival.

In the post-pandemic world, virtual communication using online tools has rapidly expanded and alternative ways of working have taken hold, and we are unlikely to go back to the old models of physical working practice. We need to embrace a new blended approach to working life that is both virtual and physical. In terms of working space, no longer are offices playing such a prominent part. In the new era the office size will be reduced, and

DOI: 10.4324/9780367280970-2

workers will use the space to catch up with each other for physical meetings when appropriate. Moreover, one of the benefits of remote delivery is that many staff prefer this mode, and with it, working patterns that support flexible working practices. Working from home and less travel means financial savings for both the individual and the company. Companies may not invest in large city centre buildings in the future and as a consequence may require smaller space from which to operate, thus making savings. This will make a team-based approach to virtual work necessary. The side effect of these changes may encourage loneliness and isolation and as such an awareness of the differing emotional needs of staff will be required in this remote flexible working era. Regular check-ins with staff will be necessary and strong emotional intelligence characteristics required to help workers communicate more effectively. The wellbeing of staff will be high on the agenda and companies must learn to create strategies for this.

A brave new world – hacking humans, surveillance capitalism and virtual ethics

Today all leaders are digital leaders, not only setting the digital strategy but anticipating the imminent changes within the context of their own sector. Added to this, are the realities of the inevitable changes occurring and the unknowable forces at work result in increasing ethical issues involving surveillance capital within our time. This leads into the inevitability of leaders needing to have a strong moral and ethical compass in decision making for the good of the company and society. How then do leaders prepare for this inevitable change? Kelly (2016) from a technology perspective discusses the relentless change and how these significant changes involve some aspect of technology. He suggests that all is flux and that nothing is finished, and nothing is done. In other words, our new brave world is in a never-ending state of change arising from the constant developments in technology. Kelly argues that it takes us a decade after new technology appears, to develop a social consensus on what this means for us, and what etiquette we need to tame this. He acknowledges that at heart we are passive, surrendering without questioning, and he calls this "the inevitable" in society. He suggests that we need to be awake and aware of this passive acceptance, in order to make more informed choices and develop a social consensus of what forms new etiquette. Consequently, etiquette needs to be a set of rules that we all agree upon.

However, Kelly's position is mild in comparison to Shoshana Zuboff's (2019) commentary. Again, from a technological position, Zuboff draws on her immense experience in this subject area and proposes that we have entered the world of surveillance capitalism. Surveillance capitalism definition highlights the coming of a new economic order that claims human experience as free raw material for translation into behavioural data, using hidden commercial practices of extraction, prediction and sales (Zuboff 2019). Zuboff emphasises that this is as significant a threat to human nature in the twenty-first century as industrial capitalism was to the natural world in the nineteenth and twentieth centuries. Zuboff views this as an overview of people's sovereignty. Zuboff points out that behavioural surplus data is fed into processes and fabricated into prediction products that anticipate what you will do now, soon and later. These predictions are traded in a new kind of marketplace that Zuboff calls behaviour futures markets. In this way, digital connection is a means to others digital ends.

At the same time, surveillance capitalists know everything about us, but their operations are designed to be unknowable. Surveillance capital is therefore unprecedented! According to Zuboff, instead of labour, surveillance capitalism feeds on every aspect of every human experience and believes our dependency is at the heart of the commercial surveillance capitalism project where there are trade-offs for effective life against the inclination to resist its bold incursions. Harari (2018) highlights that from an ethical perspective companies are heading towards tracking employees' activities and proposes that we are living in the era of hacking humans. Due to this, in the future large companies are going to be analysing and tracking your online activity by using online analytics. Consequently, surveillance capital will become the dominant form of information capitalism in our time.

Digital leaders and ethics

Ethical guidelines and behaviour are at the heart of digital behaviour and is paramount for future leaders. With the oncoming fourth and fifth generation industrial digital revolution, leaders have to make decisions about the consequences of the new technologies not only for the business but for society as a whole. Understanding and thinking through the possible scenarios that might play out and the collateral damage that may arise within society is crucial. Harari (2018) points out that whereas once nuclear war and climate change threaten only the physical survival of humankind, disruptive technologies might change the very nature of humanity and are, therefore, entangled with humans' deepest ethical and religious beliefs. Moreover, he stresses that if humankind fails to devise and administer globally accepted ethical guidelines, it will be open season for Dr Frankenstein.

Moral intelligence

Jawad and Kakabadse (2019) identify moral intelligence as MQ. They view moral intelligence as part of the five intelligences required by high-performing leaders. According to Jawad et al. the peaks and troughs of governing will continue to produce ill-conceived policies. They propose that MQ has two components: firstly, the focus on you as a person and your good intentions and values, and secondly, the demands of the situation you find yourself in. They advocate that ethical leaders exemplify private virtues, such as courage and honesty, while exercising leadership in the interest of the common good. Jawad et al. believe that morality at work translates into applied ethics, including tenure; sharing power; resisting self-aggrandising hubris; staying in touch with reality; retaining a sensible work-life balance; remembering the organisation's purpose; staying healthy; being creative; and setting aside regular time for contemplation. They also believe leaders can improve the implementation of MQ by establishing a culture of openness. Jawad et al. discuss the dilemma of leaders operating in countries where corruption is the norm. According to Jawad et al. different attitudes towards bribery, for example, create an ethical hall of mirrors and a moral maze. They highlight that in some African and South American countries such as Nigeria and Venezuela, bribery is the norm. Governments are corrupt and derive corrupt practices starting from the top and driving into the business culture itself. This suggests that assessing cross-cultural business ethics and practice is an area that needs to be openly discussed at all levels.

Corrupt practice was mentioned in the interview research with one leader highlighting the unethical international practices that they observed.

> "When I worked in the Middle East, you know, envelopes, watches, things like that can take you quite far. So, yes, I've kind of seen that happen."

> "When I worked in China, they also have various techniques. So, I was trying to sell to a business in Shanghai and they will take you out, buy you lots of alcohol, ply you with alcohol with a junior staffer and then try and negotiate. Not so much the women, more so the guys and they will do drinking games with you, try, and negotiate or they will leave it right to the last day of your trip, take you to the airport and try to negotiate knowing that you want to go home with a sale. Some of the tactics are quite dark really. They are not up front about it."
>
> Male Digital Founder

The above illustrates a type of game playing in business practice. However, it will be interesting as we move into a new virtual and digital era where the decisions are made online how this will play out. Without an appreciation of the cultural practices and differences operating across the world how then do you prepare yourself for the possibility of this happening? Bribery in certain countries according to Jawad et al. is standard practice. Dealing with countries and individuals outside of your own cultural norm could cause individual and psychological stress. Beck and Cowan (2005) help to illustrate the cultural dimension you may step into as they discuss colour-coded meme systems to help leaders navigating their way in a global marketplace. There is no doubt that moral and ethical decision-making and complexity in international markets crosses boundaries into authentic and open leadership. Making a stand in this direction is not the easy route for any leader in an increasingly volatile and complex world.

The following quotes from the qualitative research interviews emphasise that being an ethical person is walking your beliefs.

> "I think it is a matter of daily news the problems that we have in the tech industry, and a lack of moral direction."
>
> "Reputation takes years to build and no time to lose."
>
> "Well, you have got to believe in yourself, but you have also got to discipline yourself to do as you say, and to mean it. So being an ethical person and trying to do right basically is a really important thing for both the person and organisation."
>
> Male Managing Director of a digital company

Failure of character in modern society

"Do prestigious things that pay well that have no risk! Right, that is a rational philosophy of life right. That does make sense but as it turns out it is not a very great way to develop, certainly as a leader or character. I mean that's certainly something, I mean we talked about that sort of failure of character in modern society."

Male Managing Director of a digital company

"Well, I've worked with people . . . I've worked with someone who are also kind of . . . charismatic but asked me to break the law."

Male Creative Digital Founder

"I also realise that sometimes you work with senior leaders who are so self-involved and don't have a moral compass that they will throw anyone else in their way, and I know that I will never do that, and I also know that it is really difficult to be a woman in leadership, so I have used all of this experience to then try and coach and teach."

Female Senior Creative Digital Leader

"Virtual – offers the ability to manipulate and take advantage of whatever – doesn't it? Because you do not sit their face to face. It is 'faceless' leadership isn't it."

Male Leader

These leaders outline their belief that a moral ethical compass is crucial when working in a variety of situations. Developing a moral ethical compass as implied means being strong and doing what is right.

Tech savvy and strategic change

Today, leaders require a "built-in antenna" to anticipate the technological forces that may impact upon organisations, and they need to have ways of operating to anticipate change in new trends, to operate within disruptive, fast-moving environments where technology is no longer about aligning ICT (information and communication technologies) to the business, but where ICT is the business. Tech savviness involves leaders using their antennae to reimagine and predict future changes. The antenna needs to be switched on so that any new technological developments can show up on the radar allowing these threats/opportunities or new solutions to be incorporated into future thinking. Leaders need to combine this with the ability to apply strategic road-mapping to highlight the consequences of how technology and change will impact upon business and society.

Digital working practice requires a high degree of strategic direction. Digital leaders need to provide a roadmap (blueprint) for the future direction of the organisation. They need to be using their corporate business intelligence to constantly be on the lookout for rapidly changing business disruption in their sector. Bennis (2013) argues that digital business strategy is a very important issue for leadership because it is going to fundamentally change every leader's life – whatever type of institution they are leading. In terms of updating the strategic focus and considering the speed of change, Li (2020) suggests that in today's high-risk business world, leaders must learn to act quickly. According to Li, the leadership challenge is neither in developing new strategies and business models or new organizational designs enabled by digital technologies nor in effectively executing them as planned, but rather, in successfully managing the transition from where the organization is towards a desired future state. In this respect, Li argues that it is necessary to evaluate and recalibrate both the path and destination of the organisation using emerging intelligence (Li 2018a; Ross 2020). In this way, Li's research findings state that at least three new approaches are emerging in leading organizations: (1) innovating by experimenting, (2) radical transformation through successive incremental changes and (3) dynamic sustainable advantages through an evolving portfolio of temporary advantages. This challenges traditional linear approaches for leading digital transformation and highlights the need for new and iterative approaches for bridging the strategy – execution gap in the volatile digital economy (Li 2020).

The leadership interviewees mentioned that the future would be bespoke, leaders having many, many jobs in a lifetime in the "gig economy" and that there would be no stability. "It is going to be different . . . and listening is very important. The three things I have said are bespokeness, listening and accepting that the world is different," said a male Managing Director of a creative businesses. Listening through being customer-centric is highlighted in the following sections.

Being customer-centric

The new technologies have created new industries, disrupted old ones, spawned communication networks at astonishing speed, whilst global emergencies seem to erupt at ever-shorter intervals. As such, many of these developments will have profound implications for organisations and the people who lead them (McKinsey Quarterly 2012). As such, this creates a new context for leadership. Moreover, in terms of information systems, Muller (2015) emphasizes "the big shift" taking place in ICT. The shift is from inward facing ICT to outward facing ICT extending to customer empowerment. This shift could lead to a gradual transformation of the globalized consumer economy away from products and towards "experiences" in a customer-centric global economy. The consumer is focused upon the "buyer experiences" and as such the requirement of the enterprise must shift accordingly. The leader appreciates the winds of change in both physical and digital ecology where the customer is part of a dis-abandoning economy (Hjorth & Steyaert 2003), where when they are not satisfied, customers quickly disband the product or service provided. A customer-centric approaches embrace this.

Digital working – hybrid and flexible working

In the "new normal" era, growth has appeared at a rapid pace, in the form of increasing digital tech skill sets for survival. We all need to embrace ever changing skill sets and virtual tools for communicating, working, operating and collaborating in virtual space. Technology has shown us techniques that have enabled us to survive and communicate with each other in new ways both personally and professionally. Companies are emerging from the pandemic crisis, into a workplace of physical distancing where they have already made rapid changes or intend to re-imagine future operations. Yet, we are at the same time continuing with the challenges of survival at both national and international level. The era of hybrid work practice has arrived. We were practicing hybrid working before, but post pandemic this has fast tracked into the new norm rather than the exception. Along with homeworking new tech. tools skill sets have rapidly developed in a short space of time to support collaborative working practice. As such, workers have been pushed out of their comfort zone as they attempt to rapidly adjust to a new era, developing the digital expertise that goes with the practice. Work patterns have changed, and workspaces are developing and transforming as part of these changes. Thus, flexible and hybrid working practice means that all leaders and managers have to understand virtual working practice and facilitation. As such, leaders may need to appreciate the different spaces and environments in which staff are operating from, such as the formal office space, the café or homeworking with all its complexities and differences. In essence, the time element has changed, and conventional rules have been overthrown because people do not need to work the conventional nine-to-five working patterns anymore. This means new rules of working outside of the office will need to be agreed in advance. A flexible mindset is required showing understanding of the challenges of staff working from home, will be imperative. Virtual working means applying good project management and agile methods to teamwork. Appreciating the opportunities, limitations and the demands placed upon staff due to the ever-changing technologies and systems will be crucial, and this needs to be aligned to constant staff development.

Creating a culture

Culture is the life blood of an organisation. The pumping heart of the business. This may be evidenced in the whole business or found in sub-sections of the business. Culture creates a type of "collective wellbeing." Who does not want to be part of a creative culture that infuses energy and creativity between individuals? A collegiate and collaborative culture where psychological safety (Edmondson 2019) is at the heart of the culture or sub-culture of the organisations is a place where people want to work.

The culture is created by the values lived and communicated to the other members of the organisation and led by the leader. Therefore, creating culture is right at the heart of leadership. Questions include: Can we create a manual of "We" as part of this culture? Neil Crofts (2016) suggests that the results achieved by any business or team, positive or negative, are realised through the agency of the culture, and culture is defined by the leader. Culture is also created by the values lived and communicated to the other members of the organisation by the leader. Hofstede (1980) discusses values as being defined as "broad tendencies" to prefer certain states of affairs over others. In addition, culture may create the energy for a dynamic environment in which to work. Choosing the type of environment in which you wish to work can be crucial to your happiness in the workplace. Byers et al. (2015) argue that emotional engagement between people and business creates a distinctive culture. They believe a leader is a team's emotional guide who supports solid emotional intelligence, emphasising not only the emotional life but the energy of the enterprise. This energy is discussed in terms of the "entrepreneurial spirit of the team" by Soriano and Martinez (2007) which is clearly based on the relationship style of those involved. Soriano and Martinez highlight how a task-orientated leadership reduces the chance of transmitting this spirit. Creating the right conditions supports the transmission of the entrepreneurial spirit. A suitable type of leader to support this, may be one that focuses on "leadership jazz," a metaphor for creating symphonies and harmonies whilst collaboratively creating, improving and exploring new variations.

Shifting cultures and inter-cultural competence

Appreciating the culture and dynamics of the organisation that you are working in is a key factor to choosing a place to work. Working across cultural boundaries is part of hybrid working practice and this requires inter-cultural sensitivities. Trompenaars and Woolliams (2020) describe a new approach to measuring inter-cultural competence and multicultural environments. They argue that critical evaluations are not free of cultural bias and are often stuck in a time warp focussing on cultural difference rather than how to assess the competence to deal with differences. They highlight that individualism is at one end of the spectrum and collectivism is at the other, suggesting that there is a dilemma between these two seemingly opposing orientations. The response by Trompenaars and Woolliams was to assemble an Intercultural Competence Profile (ICP) assessment tool where they distinguish four aspects: recognition, respect, reconciliation and realisation. They emphasize a person's cultural differences, considering, how respectful a person is about cultural difference and respect for the value of human dignity and the recognition and acknowledgement of this in all persons. In other words, acceptance of other culture's values is important, and they propose four clusters.

The first cluster, called recognition, includes the respondents' awareness of the interconnection and change involved in nations, cultures and civilizations, including their own society and the societies of other peoples. It defines key elements of what we call a global consciousness. The second cluster, respect, includes our attitudinal, cognitive and behavioural orientation towards people that hold a diversity of values. The third cluster focuses on reconciliation, highlighting the propensity of a person to deal with differences. In particular, they believe that as a competent reconciler you must inspire as well as listen. Trompenaars and Woolliams outline three levels of reconciling including: aspects of human relations, individual creativity and team spirit, a competitive mindset and passion and control between the emotionally passionate person and those who do not display emotions, or who act like robots. They believe that reconciliation is essential between those who are purely analytical and those who are big-picture thinkers. Harmony is the later between the two aspects. Trompenaars and Woolliams believe that reconciliation is both "doing" and "being" and suggest that successful reconcilers will act the way they really are. In other words, be authentic. The fourth cluster, realisation, comprises achieving the task, managing the team or group and managing individuals.

Moreover, they propose that one of the important causes of stress is that "doing" and "being" are not integrated. They propose that the reconciling aspects of human relationships show that we need to be able to recognise individual creativity, team spirt, passion and control, analysis and big picture thinking along with "being and doing" whilst fundamentally being authentic. The new ICP inter-cultural competence assessment presented emphasises internal and external factors, the changing nature of work and the need to produce a new inter-cultural competence profile that enables us to recognise our own limitations. Trompenaars and Woolliams suggest that excessive compulsion to perform when not matched by someone's true personality, leads to ineffective behaviour. Thus, as suggested, authentic behaviour is a key aspect for resilience, and those individuals who are not in alignment with their own personal and professional values are at risk of stress in the workplace.

Cultural impacts in a digital workspace on West Coast America

Lyons (2019) discusses the distressing culture and work experience of staff in small corporate start-up companies in West Coast America. One company that Lyons observed was HubSpot. Whilst previously working there he noticed that staff felt like they had stepped inside some sort of alternative reality, where people did bad things to them for no reason. They felt helpless, powerless, confused and victimised and many questioned their sanity, whilst doubting their self-worth. They talked about what they did to me there (Lyons 2019). Taking this further, Lyons highlights that some staff in companies on the West Coast had even fantasized that their companies were not companies at all, but rather were part of some long-term psychological experiment. He was of the opinion that "the shabby treatment of employees" was not happening by accident, but rather by design, and it was happening because the new economy has been hijacked by a caste of venture capitalists and amoral founders who have taken the notion of shareholder capitalism (the idea that a company's only duty is to provide the biggest possible return to investors) and pushing that ideology to excruciatingly dangerous extremes. Lyons exposes the dark side and questions how any organisation or culture got to that place. He proposes four tech-related tendencies that contribute to worker unhappiness. They include the money and the robbery that has been carried out on workers insecurity; living in constant fear of losing the job; change and new technologies and methods in terms of how we work. Lyons believes that workers exposed to persistent, low-paid work and change leads to depression and anxiety. Lyons also found people pushing back against the changes hurting the workers and as such wreaking havoc on society, by instead focusing on a human-centred future where employees are treated with dignity and respect. The above examples emphasise the changing nature of work, the impact of the gig economy and cultural dynamics that are out of control. In the digital era, assessing the culture of any potential place you may be required to work in, may not be easy, but it is worth trying to assess before you find yourself in either a toxic workspace or a dynamic positive environment.

Summary

In the contemporary twenty-first century, cooperation, collaboration and flexible and agile conditions help the leader to ride the tides of change. The tides of change mean making complex decisions that impact on society and as such a moral ethical compass (MQ) will become an essential component of leadership. It is not enough to work alone, therefore building good relationships and trust; working in an agile flexible manner and embracing fast failure are all part of this process. It has been highlighted that authentic behaviour is a key aspect for resilience. Embracing change and keeping on top of the latest developments in technology will help future leaders plan ahead and sustain business. In this way, they create the windmills of the future that will sustain them. Future leaders need to be aware of the cultures they lead and create in multi-cultural environments and the types of characters that inhabit the culture. The contemporary leader undoubtedly needs to be a tech savvy digital leader and futurist with a high level of moral and ethical intelligence.

References

Beck D E & Cowan C C (2005) *Spiral Dynamics: Mastering Values, Leadership and Change*, Blackwell Publishing, Cambridge, MA

Bennis W (2013) Leadership in a Digital World: Embracing Transparency and Adaptive Capacity, *MIS Quarterly*, 37:2, 635–636.

Byers T, Dorf R C & Nelson A J (2015) *Technology Ventures: From Idea to Enterprise*, McGraw-Hill Publisher, New York

Crofts N (2016) https://holoschange.com/the-faculty/neil-crofts Access October 2020

Edmondson A C (2019) *The Fearless Organisation. Creating Psychological Safety in the Workplace for Leaning, Innovation and Growth*, Wiley, Hoboken, NJ

Harari Y N (2018) *21 Lessons for the 21st Century*, Penguin Random House, Vintage, London

Hjorth D & Steyaert C (2003) (3rd Edit) *Innovation and Entrepreneurship*, Wiley, Hoboken, NJ, Chapter 16

Hofstede G (1980) *Culture's Consequences: International Differences in Work-Related Values*, Sage, Beverly Hills, CA

Jawad A Q & Kakabadse A (2019) *Leadership Intelligence: The 5Qs for Thriving as a Leader*, Publisher Bloomsbury, London

Kelly K (2016) *The Inevitable: Understanding the 12 Technological Forces that Will Shape Our Future*, Viking, Random House, New York

Li (2018a); Ross (2020) Cited in Li Feng L (2020) Leading Digital Transformation: Three Emerging Approaches for Managing the Transition, *International Journal of Operations & Production Management*, 40:6, 809–817

Li Feng (2020) Leading Digital Transformation: Three Emerging Approaches for Managing the Transition, *International Journal of Operations & Production Management*, 40:6, 809–817

Lyons D (2019) *Lab Rats: Why Modern Work Makes People Miserable*, Atlantic Books, London

McKinsey Quarterly (2012) www.mckinsey.com/quarterly/overview

Muller H (2015) *The Big Shift in IT Leadership: How Great CIOs Leverage the Power of Technology for Strategic Business Growth in the Customer-Centric Economy*, Wiley Publishing, Hoboken, NJ

Soriano R S & Martinez J M C (2007) Transmitting the Entrepreneurial Spirit to the Work Team in SME's, *Management* Decisions, 45:7

Trompenaars F & Woolliams P (2020) *Cross Cultural Competence: Assessment and Diagnosis*, Adaptive Options Feature Article Publication

Young J (2018–2019) *Research Interview Insights from Resilience Study*, The Creative Digital Community, North East, UK. Research first published in this volume

Zuboff S (2019) *The Age of Surveillance Capital: The Fight for a Human Future at the New Frontier of Power*, Profile Books, Hatchette Book Group, New York, NY

3

LEADING DIGITAL TEAMS

Digital, agile and collaborative teams

Today, the knowledge era requires leaders who can inspire and empower people to be collaborative. As such, leadership power is increasingly shifting from single individuals to teams in a matrix structure. Today's leaders require a skill set inclusive of social and emotional intelligence which creates value in the form of social capital. Virtual team skill sets may include building trust, empathy, online communication skills and support to colleagues through informal communication, after action review, and of course, wellness and self-awareness. We need to put humans at the heart of innovation. In other words, soft skills are becoming far more important than ever in the virtual working environment. Digital leaders need to focus on people engagement and motivating staff in alignment with the organisational values and this can even be supported through the latest software. Feedback from the interviewees confirms this.

DOI: 10.4324/9780367280970-3

Here, one leader is talking about using the latest software to prompt ways of operating:

> *"So, by producing the people engagement software we've looked at, it actually alerts you to when you should be giving that person a pat on the back, you should be saying thank you, you should be doing these things. You should be giving them a reward, you should . . . and it allows them to do all of that from a platform, or from their phone."*
>
> Male Managing Director

"None are as smart as all of us," Bennis & Ward

Business guru, Warren Bennis in Bennis and Ward Biederman (1997) showed wisdom by focusing attention on team leadership, rather than charismatic individual leadership, and in doing so offered a model for global business of the future. According to Bennis, great groups are formed within dynamic dedicated teams. Leaders of these teams provide direction and meaning and a sense of purpose, and they generate and sustain trust in order to create authentic relationships. He believes they display a bias towards risk-taking and curiosity, and as purveyors of hope, they create the environment and culture around them. Colleagues will rely on leaders if they show authentic behaviour and psychologically show a type of optimism that helps to shelter others and create success. Bennis helps us to understand the "multiplier effect" of the many, which can be created when working in great teams. The multiplier effect underscores collective intelligence that can increase the fruits of our work.

Creating digital teams and working on projects

In the digital era, flexibility, agility, experimentation and feedback from the customer will enable success. Thus, methods used to do this may include the application of the lean start-up theory (Ries 2011), customer development and design thinking. These working practices include agile ways of working; testing hypothesis; customer focused feedback; iterative design; visual working and embracing fast failure. Part of the process is listening to customer feedback (Blank 2012) in order to pivot or persevere. Business models have become more visual, via for instance, the Business

Model Canvas (Osterwalder & Pigneur 2012), as they encourage the team to get together to test out hypotheses, evaluate feedback and change the business model quickly when necessary. In this way, instead of a long-term and static approach to business planning, a visual design approach can be embraced by leaders, who can regularly update the plan through customer feedback, whilst at the same time constantly using their strategic antenna to be on their guard. These are all strategies used by the digital entrepreneur.

Innovative methodologies

With increasing digital working practice and the hybrid nature of work, companies are now creating agile networks and teams. Because of this, the recent trends are for real time feedback through contemporary project management practices such as Scrum (Sutherland 2015). Agile methods for software development, such as Scrum are often team-based, iterative and rely on collaborative, self-organising teams to dynamically adjust to changing customer requirements, needing to balance freedom and responsibility, learning and performance (Hoda et al. 2010). The formal leadership role becomes more informal in this context essentially with a collective capacity for change in complex context. Sutherland took inspiration for Scrum project management practices from the work of two famous Japanese/America professors Takeuchi and Nonaka (1986) in their paper called, "The new product development game." The Scrum theory is organised around prioritised projects and introduces small cross functional teams setting up weekly sprints to hold everyone to account whilst conducting brief daily stand-ups (daily meetings where everyone stands up for the duration of the very short meeting to discover problems, focus on continuous improvement, bursts of inspiration and immediate feedback). Sprints and daily feedback practice for all participants are facilitated by a scrum master (guide and leader). The team encourages diversity of skill set, thinking and experience and cross-functional working practices as they work on whole projects. These techniques are perhaps even more significant when working on projects in digital teams in an online ecology. This type of leadership is seen as key in balancing freedom and alignment as demanded in highly dynamic contexts. The AC (Agile coach) as a complexity leader values being present, observing and reacting in the moment.

Fast failure and learning

How you respond to failure has a huge effect on bounce back at both the organisational and individual level. For Bennis, the most impressive and memorable quality of individuals in his study was how to respond to failure. He highlights that they do not think about failure or use the word! It is about mind-set and lessons learnt (Bennis & Ward Biederman 1997). Ries (2011) proposed fast failure as a principle of the lean start-up methodology for entrepreneurs. Whilst Kouzes and Posner (2007) suggest that learning can also come from reflecting on failures: "Life is the leader's laboratory, and exemplary leaders use it to conduct as many experiments as possible." Olsen (2014) adds that we should remember that any successful political leader, artist, scientist or Olympic athlete has had many failures and suggests that what separates the leaders are those that learn from their difficulties, make adjustments, and go on. Like bamboo, they bend, but do not break. Persevering, they stay the course to reach the finish line. The question is, when is failure real failure or is it just part of the learning process? Entrepreneurs and intrapreneurs in companies have learnt to significantly value all failure but it is the speed of a fast failure mentality that helps the enterprising leader to succeed.

The data highlighted that it was only from failure that real learning took place. Try, fail, learn. The assumption is that this learning is deep learning and forms part of a growth mindset.

> *"People always say that in failure, the real learning happens."*
>
> Male Managing Director of a digital company.

> "How do we move from thinking that if we fail at something that we are a failure and, therefore, are beyond redemption? So, part of it is having a growth mindset in which feedback is useful for learning. So, if we fail at things, then actually, its's giving us a signal and how can we learn from that."
>
> "My guess is that life is a process of continual experimentation and continual knock backs and it's like how do we actually create more, like a growth mindset, so that all the feedback we get is part of that learning process. It starts when we are born and it finishes when we die and, basically, doing that all the time. So, how can we get used to that meta-model of just that learning all the time?"
>
> Male Creative Digital Founder

As part of the above, an appreciation of cross-function teamwork is important as many leaders lead or participate in various teams. With this in mind, good project management skills, time management and an ability to apply soft collaborative skills will become increasingly important.

Creating trusting relationships

How do you operate effectively within teams in the virtual workplace? Although we are visually seeing each other, the distributed nature and lack of face-to-face activity can have its own problems. In discussing distributed teamwork, the paradox of trust at a general level, the phenomenon of trust can be described as "a willingness of a party to be vulnerable to actions of another party based on the expectations that the other will perform a particular action important to the trustor, irrespective of the ability to monitor or control that other party" (Mayer et al. 1995). This is often described as the "paradox of trust."

Relationships and building trust

The concept of trust is a main tenet for relationships in organisations, and this is what enables effective communication and knowledge sharing. Abrahams et al. (2003) emphasise that "interpersonal trust" can be defined as the "willingness of a party" to be vulnerable. According to Abrahams et al. "benevolence-based trust" allows one to query a colleague in depth without fear of damage to self-esteem or reputation. Abrahams argues that leaders must trust that the people they have to turn to, to have sufficient expertise to offer solutions. Whilst "competence-based trust" allows one to feel confident that the person sought out knows what he/she is talking about and is worth listening to and learning from. Developing trusting relationships leads to high levels of intangible asset creation.

Julsrud and Bakke (2010) in their empirical Nordic study recognise the importance of trustful ties that cross boundaries and countries. They take a relational approach to trust and recognize the importance of trust as generated through individuals that have created trustful ties across central boundaries, known as trust brokers. As such, these brokers establish trust quickly. Two elements they identify are *cognitive dimension* and *affected-based* trust. The *cognitive dimension* refers to the calculative and rational characteristics demonstrated by trustees, such as reliability, integrity, competence and responsibility. *Affected based trust*, on the other hand involves emotional elements and the social skills of those trusted. The concept of trust brokering addresses two central issues: the establishment of trustful relationships and the "bridging" of formerly weakly connected group or sub-groups within a larger structured network. A trust broker may be seen as an individual that actively seeks to establish trustful ties across groups with low levels of trust, whereas trust brokerage may be seen as the outcome of trust brokering activities. Granovetter (1973), argues that the strength of ties is the outcome of the combination of the amount of time, the emotional intensity, the intimacy, mutual confiding and the reciprocal services characterized by the tie. Whilst Mayer et al. (1995) propose three central factors that influence the general trustworthiness of a person: ability, benevolence and integrity. In this way, the trustworthiness of a certain person builds on how a trustor understands a person's particular – competence, intentions and personal integrity. Once more, competence, benevolence, kindness and integrity are the baseline of trust in relationships and a trust broker leads in this direction. Being able to respect your leader whether the CEO or the project manager is a really important issue for most individuals, and this is even more so in a virtual environment.

To build trust in the future it will be necessary to engage in continuous and frequent interaction of some form to help maintain trust. The management style to foster trust will include support for the team, measuring outputs rather than process and paying attention to a range of stakeholders to maintain their confidence and trust. In addition, communication allows you maintain motivation by talking regularly with other team members both formally and informally.

This Chief Executive discusses the power of the team and the trust issues involved in leading the team.

> *"Well that's really important, that's the power of your team because you want them to put trust in you and you want them to feel that they've always got your back and you want your team to know that you do listen to them and you do listen to their ideas. I mean this team is really close and really tight, as I say they haven't been together that long, but they're functioning really well."*
>
> Male Chief Executive of a creative business

Psychological safety

When working in teams in the workplace, members perform better when they feel secure and safe in the environment in which they work. Project members work best together when they trust other members of the team and the culture created within the team. There is a need to create psychological safety for individuals so that members of a team feel secure and capable of making changes. Edmondson (1999) proposed in her early research work based on a study of 51 teams that team psychological safety is defined as a shared belief that the team is safe for interpersonal risk taking. Edmondson (2019) also broadly defined psychological safety as a climate in which people are comfortable expressing and being themselves, and a place where colleagues feel comfortable sharing concerns and mistakes without fear of embarrassment or retribution. Psychological safety ensures a sense of confidence that the team will not embarrass, humiliate, ignore, reject or punish someone for speaking up. In this safe environment team members know they can ask questions and they tend to trust colleagues. This confidence stems from mutual respect and trust among team members. Edmondson (2019) argues that whether you are teaming with new colleagues all the time or working in a stable team, effective teamwork happens best in a psychologically safe workplace. She highlights that psychological safety is not immunity from consequence nor is it being held in high regard. In psychologically safe workplaces people know they might fail or receive performance feedback that states they are not meeting expectations, or that they might lose their jobs due to change. However, in safe environments, people are not hindered by interpersonal fear, and feel willing and able to take the inherent interpersonal risks of candour. As such, in the fearless organisation (Edmondson 2019) inter-personal fear is minimised so that the team and organisational performance can be maximised in a knowledge intensive world. De-stigmatizing and reframing failure create forums for input and discussion and brainstorming. As we step into the digital i-connected world it is important to feel safe enough within the culture to admit mistakes so that they can be rectified quickly and promptly. In an environment rapidly moving into virtual working practice the need for a team culture where members practice psychological safety and set expectations about failure and uncertainty sets the stage so that members can learn from mistakes (at speed).

An example of this is discussed by this leader.

Psychological safety (in organisational culture)

"My belief is that the capstone of any corporate culture is psychological safety. So, actually, the key thing is psychological safety and do people feel safe to take inter-personal risks?"

"So, harmony is essential. But, so, my colleague . . . talks about enough safety. So, this is about psychological safety. So, I think that if one is being entrepreneurial and taking risks then harmony is vital, but I would reframe it with the concept of psychological safety which is related but different. So, harmony – you will always have conflict, but it's actually how can you deal with differences of opinion in a constructive way so that people can have those discussions."

Male Creative Digital Founder

Psychologically safe environments create an underpinning ethos to counteract fear, reframe failure and help organisations to learn, grow and ultimately innovate through ambiguity.

Building and identifying social capital in a virtual world

Leaders need to increase the serendipity and inter-connectedness of the team when they interact online. Finding ways to do this is very important in the post-pandemic workplace where increasingly the default is virtual working practice. As discussed above, building relationships and trust is at the heart of this process and encouraging honest, open, seamless, authentic communication is part of this process. Moreover, value creation is social in nature and embedded in social relations and the way systems organise themselves. An awareness of social capital as an organisational asset that is social and relational in nature, and that can be exploited, is crucial for the contemporary organisations. Nahapiet and Ghoshal (1998) view social capital as a relational resource. They propose that the social capital label encompasses the actual and potential resources embedded within, available through, and derived from the "network of relationships" possessed by an individual or social unit. Whilst for McKelroy (2003) there are two major schools of thought, namely, "egocentric" and "socio-centric" perspectives. He suggests that an "egocentric" perspective is a useful label to attach to social capital creation and arises within online environments. McElroy believes that individual relationships are important as it is the development of these relationships inclusive of trust, reciprocity and shared values that help individuals open up, in order to share knowledge and ideas with one another. In terms of relationships, Nahapiet and Ghoshal (1998) and McKelroy (2003) discuss social capital under the intellectual capital umbrella. Social capital arises online as members share their mental models, reflect and gain ideas and insight generated from the conversation in order to reinforce those ideas. Strong ties support highly developed social capital and higher social coherence whilst weak ties are important but lead to less social coherence.

Appreciating where social capital resides in the business is key to identifying value, particularly in the digital business. The question may be: Where is the "intangible value"? Essential amongst this is knowing and identifying the individuals who become trust brokers who build strong relationships in the virtual collaborative environment. Moreover, social capital innovation is a valuable (albeit intangible resource) in a world where distributed virtual working practice is mainstream. Thus, in the current context it is important to understand who the knowledge and trust brokers are, and who is leading with integrity. These will be the individuals and leaders that you turn to when in need.

Living and working in the ba space

Digital leaders undoubtedly need to learn to dive in and out of physical and virtual space in this new era. In addition, adding the individual mental internal space – and you have understood the concept of a hybrid space called ba (Nonaka & Takeuchi 1998), a concept to support the interactions and knowledge sharing that occurs to support knowledge creation. Leaders are creating knowledge within the boundaries of ba inclusive of interacting in virtual, physical and mental space. The ba terminology can be viewed as a metaphor for places and spaces that allow us to understand the mechanisms by which we reach out, develop and interact with one another. Ba is also conceived as the frame (made up of borders of space and time) in which knowledge is activated as a resource for knowledge creation that is intangible, boundaryless and dynamic. Never has ba been so important as we currently dive in and out of virtual digital and physical space, and at the same time interacting in mental ba at all times. This is a complex multi-layered ecology that operates with multiple levels encompassing both inner mental space, external virtual space (cyber ba) and real-world physical space (within an interacting or dialoguing ba) Nonaka et al. (2000). Thus, this dynamic process of creating new knowledge spirals emerges in a complex arena of spaces. More focus is required on all forms of ba, considering the emerging new technologies and the array of new tools being used. Key, is an appreciation of the complexity of the dynamic ecology we now work in.

Creating communities of practice

Another mechanism for communicating within an organisation or across the globe is to build communities of practice (Wenger 2000; Wenger et al. 2002). Communities of practice or (interest or passion) can be formal or informal self-evolving communities, or they can be managed communities top-down or bottom up. Communities of practice (COPs) can also be created in physical or virtual space. Within a community there are elements of acceptance, so that acceptance into the community means acknowledgement of a member's area of expertise. Acceptance plays a key part where the (practice or passion, interest and expertise) of those entering the domain is validated by other members. Within a virtual community, dialogue is encouraged, enabling ideas and reflective thoughts to be bounced around in order to support the emergence of new views (Young 2012). Those communities that self-evolve can be disruptive for the organisation as the structure of command and control is penetrated by the members of the community who may span across the organisation hierarchy by sharing a common interest. On the other hand, the community share knowledge, insights and ideas and as such come together to create synergies within their learning community, building potentially interesting outcomes and social capital whilst at the same time sharing their expertise and collaborating on important issues. These outcomes can be viewed as social assets that can be developed to create a collaborative spirit and support learning in organisations. The virtual community of practice is even more important in the present climate within a hybrid working environment. New knowledge can be created from a collaborative, social, individualistic and dynamic perspective. COPs help build relationship that expand boundaries, disrupt the status quo, create synergy and share expertise and learning amongst experts in an area of interest.

With both hybrid and e-working practice, virtual communities of practice have fully arrived to share knowledge, make change and disrupt.

Strategies for virtual working

As we move into a time where there are more virtual and hybrid working practice, leaders need to consider implementing strategies for wellbeing and resilience in the workplace. This involves creating a culture that embraces new and creative ways of operating. First this may involve creating online mentors and coaches for new staff to help them settle into the culture by encouraging project leaders to use their coaching skill set on the team. Secondly, this may also involve creating social online space for dialogue and discussion in a virtual communities that may enable staff to connect to each other, drop in talk to each other like they would in the office around the water cooler. Additionally, creating a type of digital detox agenda online may involve putting on workshops for wellbeing to encourage colleagues to take exercise daily, and possibly walk while talking online. This could include a social budget for staff whereby remote parties are orchestrated, staff sent on the virtual cocktail making workshops and charitable fund raising through walking and talking. Moreover, letting staff who work virtually know that the company encourages flexibility and shows awareness of a different set of needs. By implementing these strategies management would be reinforcing a culture of wellbeing from the top.

Global and human communication

Why send your employees on a flight across the world when you can quickly use the latest tech tools to have the conversation. The resource savings are high for the employee. However, staff will need to be proficient at appreciating the various styles of communication and nuances used in different parts of the world. Leaders will therefore need to acquire the necessary skill set to operate within different cultures. This means appreciating that what is acceptable in one culture is not in another. Awareness of online facial nuances may also be a necessary skill for digital leaders. One such mechanism is to study facial expressions (Eckman 2004). Appreciating what these expressions mean can be very insightful when reading other people's reactions especially in virtual space. Therefore, with global and digital communication and the present-day pace of change, organisations will need to reshape their learning and development to support this constant change and prepare employees for constant micro-learning with the online resources to support this. Petrucci and Rivera (2018) suggest that millennials and i-Gen (internet) generations learn differently from previous generations and, as such, prefer personalised content. In this sense they want personalisation with visual communication.

We have learnt from our recent Covid isolation experiences that to survive we need to connect online. Humans are social creatures, and it is not normal to self-isolate. We do need to reach out to others to communicate in various virtual formats. How we communicate and operate online becomes even more vital. It is so obvious when someone is cold and lifeless in their communication. A lack of warmth online is not endearing to anyone and will not attract others to you. Leaders in virtual mode still need followers. How do you connect to make sure that you have followers? Virtual characteristics are still very similar to physical attributes. For instance, as discussed above, the need to build trust in relationships becomes imperative. Trust is also built up over time – it is not a given – and the time element is important in the mix. Trust is the heart of a good relationship and relationships form part of social capital building which comes under the intellectual capital umbrella. Social capital is therefore a requirement for knowledge-focused leader in the twenty-first century.

> *"You should be giving that person a pat on the back; you should be saying thank you; you should be doing these things and you should be giving them a reward – and it allows them to do all of that from a platform or phone."*
>
> Male Managing Director

Working online may mean the loss of the "water cooler" talk in the office and with it the ability to read full body language. However, virtual working practice may now include reading of face-to-face cues and facial expressions, but additionally, using empathy and emotional intelligence and working on the informal conversation as part of social capital building. Digital leaders need to be involved in people engagement to motivate staff.

Summary

Within this chapter we have discussed working collaboratively in digital teams and the multiplier effect this creates in terms of the outputs achieved.

We have highlighted the importance of a fast failure mentality and emphasised the importance of creating psychological safety to create a safe work environment and collaborative culture. The creation of ba has been highlighted as we develop new ways of working in hybrid workspaces and additionally this may also include creating and interacting in virtual communities of practice. To move forward it is important to build and develop relationships built on trust as this supports resilience by enabling the leader to reach out to a network of trusted experts when necessary.

References

Abrahams L C, Cross R, Lesser E & Levin D Z (2003) Nurturing Interpersonal Trust in Knowledge-sharing Networks, *Academy of Management Executives*, 17:4

Bennis W & Ward Biederman P (1997) *Organising Genius. The Secrets of Creative Collaboration*, Basic Books, New York

Blank S (2012) *The Four Steps to the Epiphany: Successful Strategies for Products That Win*, K&S Ranch Publishing, Pescadero, CA; Wiley, Hoboken, NJ

Blank S & Dorf B (2012) *The Startup Owner's Manual: The Step-by-Step Guide for Building a Great Company*, John Wiley & Sons, Hoboken, NJ; K&S Ranch Publishing, Pescadero, CA

Eckman P (2004) *Emotions Revealed*, Henry Holt & Company Inc, New York

Edmondson A C (1999) Psychological Safety and Learning Behaviour in Work Teams, *Administrative Science Quarterly*, 44:2, June, 350–383

Edmondson A C (2019) *The Fearless Organisation. Creating Psychological Safety in the Workplace for Leaning, Innovation and Growth*, Wiley, Hoboken, NJ

Granovetter M S (1973) The Strength of Weak Ties, *American Journal of Sociology*, 81, 1287–1203, p. 136

Hoda Noble & Marshall (2010) Cited in Bäcklander G (2019) Doing Complexity Leadership Theory: How Agile Coaches at Spotify Practise Enabling Leadership, *Creativity and Innovation Management*, 28, 42–60

Julsrud T E & Bakke J W (2008) *Building Trust in Networked Environments: Understanding the Importance of Trust Brokers.* Cited in Brennan L L and Johnson V E (Ed) *Computer-Mediated Relationships and Trust: Managerial and Organisational Effects*, IGI Global doi 10.4018/978-1-5990-495-8

Kouzes and Posner (2007) Cited in Olsen P E (2014) Namaste: How Yoga Can Inform Leadership Education, *Journal of Leadership Education*, 13, 116, Winter 2014

Mayer R C, Davis J H & Schoorman D F (1995) An Integrative Model of Organizational Trust, *The Academy of Management Review*, 20:3, 709–734

McKelroy M W (2003) *The New Knowledge Management. Complexity, Learning and Sustainable Innovation*, Butterworth Heinemann, Oxford and New York

Nahapiet J & Ghoshal S (1998) Social Capital, Intellectual Capital and the Creation of Value in Firms, *Academy of Management*, 23:2

Nonaka I & Takeuchi H (1998) *The Knowledge-Creating Company*, Oxford University Press, Oxford

Nonaka, I, Toyama R & Konno N (2000) SECI, Ba and Leadership: A Unified Model of Dynamic Knowledge Creation, *Long Range Planning*, 33, 5–4

Olsen P E (2014) Namaste: How Yoga Can Inform Leadership Education, *Journal of Leadership Educationv*, 13, 116, Winter 2014

Osterwalder A and Pigneur Y (2012) *Business Model Generation: A Handbook for Visionaries, Game Changers and Challengers*, Strategyzer Series, Wiley, Hoboken, NJ

Petrucci T & Rivera M (2018) Leading Growth Through the Digital Leader, *Journal of Leadership Studies*, 12:3

Ries E (2011) *Lean Startup. How Constant Innovation Creates Radically Successful Business*, Penguin Random House, London

Sutherland J (2015) *SCRUM: The Art of Doing Twice the Work in Half the Time*, Random House, Penguin Publishers, London

Takeuchi H & Nonaka I (1986) The New Product Development Game, *Harvard Business Review* Jan–Feb 137–146

Wenger E (2000) Communities of Practice and Social Leaning Systems, *Organisation*, 7:2, 225–246

Wenger E, McDermott R & Snyder W M (2002) *Cultivating Communities of Practice*, Harvard Business School Press, Boston, MA

Young J (2012) *Personal Knowledge Capital: The Inner and Outer Path of Knowledge Creation in a Web World*, Chandos/Elsevier Publishers, Oxford

Young J (2018–2019) *Research Interview Insights from Leadership Resilience Study*, The Creative Digital Community, North East, UK. Research first published in this volume

4

EXPLORING PERSONAL RESILIENCE (PRQ) BY RIDING THE WAVES

Leaders – riding the waves

Today's leaders may find themselves riding a tsunami! The tsunami crashes in, destroys, changes and disrupts. In the midst of continuous change and technological disruption, the key word is survival. What does riding the waves mean? It means riding whatever sweeping changes are thrown at the business, such as global terrorism, pandemics, economic downturns and acknowledging and preparing for megatrends such as digitisation, ageing, climate change and social transformation. How leaders respond to continuous change and unpredictable challenges is key to their survival. We all need to understand the elements that make up resilience and discover what parts work for us. Indeed, resilience can be worked on and developed. Hence, finding ways to do this and becoming pre-emptive and preventative is crucial.

The mystery of resilience

There is an argument that resilience can be learned and there is an argument that whilst older people become resilient over time, younger people need to

DOI: 10.4324/9780367280970-4

learn how to be resilient. However, the argument that individual resilience is learnt over time and increases with age and experience, is not necessarily the case for older workers because we all have individual experiences, some easier than others. As such, resilience is a mystery. Resilience is an intriguing yet elusive concept: intriguing because it can provide an answer as to why one person crumbles in the face of tough times while another gains strength from them (Neenan 2018). Neenan highlights that resilience remains something of a puzzle. He quotes the philosopher Tom Morris who states that if you live long enough, "you may come to understand one of the deepest truths about life: inner resilience is the secret to outer results in the world. Challenging times demand inner strengths and a spirit that won't be defeated" (Morris 2004).

For Bennis (2013) resilience is coming back effectively and rebounding from difficult adversity. For many, resilience may be a person's ability to bounce, grow, connect and flow. Sonnenfeld and Ward (2017) suggest that for some leaders challenging and painful catastrophic defeat energises them to re-join the fray with greater determination. Coutu (2017) acknowledges that resilience is the skill and capacity to be robust under conditions of enormous stress and change. However, Coutu observes from research that resilient people possess three characteristics: a staunch acceptance of reality; a deep belief often buttressed by strongly held values that life is meaningful; and an ability to improvise. She points out that in terms of acceptance of reality, that in some circumstances rose coloured thinking can spell disaster. Accordingly, prepare in advance for the reality and ask questions such as: Do I really truly understand the situation? Can be very useful. The second point helps support the view that making decisions that bring meaning and purpose in life helps assist resilience. The third characteristic falls into the category of bricolage ("bouncing back") defined as a kind of inventiveness, an ability to improvise a solution or problem to get things done.

Tapping into and learning from life experience

Learning from life experiences is central to knowing who you are and your development and effectiveness as a leader. "If people are capable of learning from their experiences, they can acquire leadership," Northouse (2018) concluded. The following are quotes from a serial entrepreneur acknowledging how an acceptance of reality, the impact of major life experiences, add to their knowledge so that they learn from this in a positive way. Internal factors include your own individual and unique past experiences.

> "I am equally of the view that everyone has their own pain and suffering regardless, and it is easy to say and become flippant and go 'Well that person's worse off,' or 'Look at that person, they haven't got anything compared to you', or whatever. Because that doesn't really help you at all. It is about sympathising with people, because everyone has their own trials and tribulations, and it doesn't matter how rich or poor or whatever their circumstances are. They have their own issues, and you cannot compare that person to that person. Everyone is unique!"
>
> "I'm not uncomfortable with the thought of starting again if I had to tomorrow, I'd start all over again. I'd do it. I mean, there's plenty of experiences that I wish hadn't happened, but at the same time I'm not unhappy with the fact that they did, because I learned so much from them."
>
> "And going back to my point about the 'life experiences' that have sort of shaped me and made me who I am – a lot of them have not been great. They've been quite significantly bad. But it's what you do with that and how you react to them and things like that."
>
> Serial Entrepreneur

The main point here is the uniqueness of each individual, in how they respond to stress and adversity. The capacity to rebound from adversity arises in many shapes and forms as each individual reacts differently to a situation and context. Crucial is the ability to process life experiences and learn from those experiences. Moreover, we all have a variety of past experiences, in life and in business, that enable us to navigate our way in the world, and all these past experiences can be revaluated and applied to new contexts and decisions. Experience counts.

Fighting back and using emotional intelligence (EQ)

In every culture and every era, the story of the hero myth arises in leadership! Sonnenfield and Ward (2017) take an emotional intelligence and practical practitioner perspective that includes a study of 300 leaders. From this study they deduced that leaders could triumph over tragedy, provided they take conscious steps to do so. They highlight that among the test of a leader, few are more challenging – and more painful – than recovering from a career catastrophe, whether it is caused by natural disaster, illness, misconduct, slip-ups or unjust conspiratorial overthrow. For this reason, they propose that real leaders do not cave in, because defeat energizes them to re-join the fray with greater determination and vigour. They question what prevents a leader from coming back is a tendency to blame themselves and that they tend to dwell on the past rather than look to the future – in essence, secretly holding themselves responsible for their setbacks whether true or not, whilst holding on to the belief that they must carefully decide how to fight back. Once the decision has been made on how to respond to a career disaster, the question of whether to confront the situation that brought them down (an exhausting expensive, embarrassing battle) or, to try to put it behind them, leading to a graceful retreat. In discussing getting beyond rage and denial, Sonnenfield et al. suggest that the most important steps on the route to recovery is to confront and acknowledge failure. Therefore, they propose trying to understand the Machiavellian politics of others to help you rebuild your career. Their first suggestion is that you should remember that failure is a beginning, not an end, and that comeback is possible. Secondly, they propose looking to the future because pre-emptive actions are often more effective than reactive ones – even if this means standing back and reflecting on what to do next. Thirdly, they suggest helping the people around you to deal with your failure by letting them know you are ready for their assistance. Additionally, get friends and acquaintances to support you. Fourthly, they suggest, know your narrative, as reputation building involves telling and re-telling your story to get your account of events out. The final point is part of brand reputation and being keenly aware of the story and counter story. Looking to the future involves keeping a positive mind-set, whilst at the same time processing the circumstances and reflecting deeply on the next plan. However, being ready for assistance means reaching out externally for support to help you change the internal story that you tell yourself. Overall, do not make hasty decisions but rather quietly reflect on the scenarios before deciding what to do next.

The new psychology of positive emotions

Alleviating constant stress requires different tactics for different people. One action involves developing a positive attitude as a type of psychological resilience. In the psychology of positivity, Seligman (2011) and Fredrickson (2009) discuss taking positive steps mentally to encourage change and create a positive mind-set. They both discuss an array of techniques that can deliberately counteract negativity as part of building resilience through a positive cognitive intervention. Positive psychologist Seligman (2011)) asks the question, "what is it that allows us to flourish?" In doing so, wellbeing takes the stage, front and centre. Happiness (or positive emotion) becomes one of the five pillars of positive psychology, along with engagement, meaning, accomplishment and positive relations. The first, positive emotion, emphasises pleasure, comfort and warmth; the second, engagement, is about going with the flow. The third is looking for deeper meaning; the fourth and fifth, positive relationships, meaning and accomplishment, both have objective and subjective components. Additionally, Seligman includes the degree to which you meet your goals, and where these goals stand in relation to their impact on the people you care about and the world around you. Tugade and Fredickson (2004), also from a psychological research perspective, explored the impact of positive emotions on personal resilience. They found that high-resilient individuals tend to experience positive emotions even amidst stress. Proposing that two co-existing pre-conditions describe resilient individuals, where the first is the ability to recognise the effects of a stressful situation and the second to experience positive outcomes despite adversity. An important finding in Tugade and Fredrickson's research was that positive emotions contribute to the ability of resilient individuals to physiologically recover from negative emotional arousal. In this way, cardiovascular reactivity occasioned by negative emotional states of hostility, anger and anxiety plays an important role in the aetiology of cardiovascular diseases such as coronary heart disease and essential hypertension. Therefore, sustained experiences of negative emotional arousal have been shown to be associated with long-term cardiovascular illness and disease. As a consequence, it seems especially useful to understand how positive emotions might contribute to the prevention of cardiovascular disease, and how the mind processes negative circumstances.

Additionally, Tugade and Fredrickson propose that the broad and build theory proposed by Fredrickson (1998, 2001) tends to encourage and maintain positive emotions and acts as a resource to buffer against the advancement of disease and death. They argue that positive emotions are not automatic, but they can be worked on by applying the theory. Importantly, they also add, that individuals with greater tendencies to use humour in order to cope, often have a stronger immune system. From the research we can hear the views of the creative leaders. Positive emotions, as part of positive psychology, play their part in the psychological make-up of individuals with regard to resilience.

A positive mindset

> *"So, there is this concept of positive psychology with the 3:1 ratio, so three positives for every negative. That seems to open up people's thinking and they are more able to be creative; they have a wider perspective on things. That was definitely the case with CPCR, it was a very creative business."*
>
> Male International Coach and Consultant

Here is a leader describing the types of leaders with positive energy who inspired him:

Positive energy

> *"The second notion of inspiring for me is about people that have such energy. I wouldn't go so far as to say charisma because it is more nebulous, but its positive energy; they have such positive energy, and they are a joy being around and I want to spend time in their presence. Just as I don't want to spend time in the presence of people who suck my energy."*
>
> Male, experienced Creative Digital Executive Coach

Positive psychologists emphasise the need to think in a positive light and to see the positive in the situations that you encounter. Of course, this must be genuine, as well as a deliberate process of thinking. Contagion happiness and the upward spiral of positive emotions are part of this theory. Future leaders need to take note and become aware of the five pillars that will bring about the best in staff and cultivate a positive energy for themselves and within the organisation for wellbeing. Alleviating stress does mean different things for different people, however, adding a positive attitude is a psychological type of resilience that provides a buffer against stressful times follow the energy.

Evaluate and manage your psychological assets – build a bank of positivity!

Are you valuing positivity as a currency around you? Kopans (2017) argues that managers understand the clear-eyed analysis – that both quantitative and qualitative elements are essential for building a resilient business. However, they propose that we rarely apply this methodological approach. Kopans suggests that you can evaluate, manage and strengthen your own resilience in the same way that you would a company. He talks about building up your "positivity currency" that is grounded in positive interactions, events and memories. This is because a positive attitude and expressing gratitude have real value in building resilience. Kopans believes that creating a positive currency can decrease anxiety, reduce symptoms of illness and improve the quality of sleep, as a consequence, leading to greater personal resilience. By being positive we encourage others to do the same and this creates a virtuous "reverse run on the bank" and a positive feedback loop. Whilst Zehira and Narcıkarab (2016) consider that one of the most important concepts of Positive Organizational Behaviour is Psychological Capital. The integration of hope, efficacy, resilience and optimism represents the core construct of PsyCap. This PsyCap is identified by these four positive psychological resources (Avey et al. 2010) and characterized by: (1) having confidence (self-efficacy) to take responsibility and achieve challenging tasks; (2) making a positive attribution (optimism) about succeeding now and in the future; (3) persevering toward goals and, when necessary, redirecting paths to goals (hope); and (4) when the problem occurs, sustaining and bouncing back and even beyond (resilience) to attain success (Luthans et al. 2007). Positive assets are often forgotten as they are intangible assets that need to be valued by leaders and organisations.

The following Managing Director emphasises his use of the emotional bank and uses the analogy of going into debt. Whilst at the same time shows his use of positive psychology techniques by evaluating challenges in terms of the meaning derived from them and so turning the negative into a positive. From the interview research we can hear the views of the creative leaders in terms of exploring positive emotions and a positive outlook and how this can produce an upward, positive spiral.

The emotional bank

> "Positivity from the emotional bank! I call it my emotional bank account because that is where the positivity is . . . that is where all the credits are, based on reality. So, in times when you are going into debt you need more credit."

> "I always look at all the things that go negative to become a catalyst for something new. I think if you do not look at them as an opportunity rather than a negative then you will struggle. Being an entrepreneur, one of the lessons I take away is not to get too high when things are going well, and I am not going to get too low when things are not going my way. A lot of entrepreneurs do, and they are on an emotional roller-coaster."
>
> Male Managing Director

Kopans (2017) suggests taking a portfolio approach so that individuals increase resilience by evaluating what it is that provides the "highest returns" across an entire life portfolio. He argues that by generating more positive currency in those areas, you will increase the ability to bring the best of yourself to work. He believes that we all need to regularly review our own positivity currency. This enables corrective action when necessary and gleans insight, in order to boost your positivity by increasing exposure to positive interactions and expressions of gratitude. The Managing Director's quote supports the view that we should make it a habit to find time to regularly evaluate our own emotional bank account.

Integral solutions for resilience

In a report by Hansen at the Resilience Institute based on 21,239 respondents in 2018, Hansen reported how resilience assessment diagnostic tools were applied across the world in five languages and the outcomes highlighted that humans are an integral mix of physical, emotional, and cognitive attributes recommending integral solutions. They saw the following as high score assets (master stress; energise body; engage emotion, train mind, spirit in action) as signs of resilience, whilst low liability scores included being (depressed, distressed, vulnerable, withdrawn, disengaged and confused). In this report the key liability factors were fatigue, intensity, worry, being self-critical, overload, apathy, chronic symptoms, sloth, self-doubt, and hypervigilance. A main feature was that resilience interventions programmes deliver multiple benefits for the individual and organisation, including reducing risk (safety, mental health, illness and conflict) and increasing performance (physical, emotional and mental). The integral solution led by international feedback is undoubtedly a rounded approach to individual resilience. This integral view is multi-faceted and focuses on more than one aspect of resilience. It fits with a mind-body-spirit approach to resilience, rather than a silo approach.

Re-charging – recovery time, alignment and balance

The ability to recover from or adjust easily to misfortune or change (the bounce back/forward capability) also relates to a time element involved in resilience. A resilient person is well rested, and overwork and exhaustion are the opposite of resilience. From an emotional intelligence perspective, Anchor and Gielan (2017) believe a lack of a recovery period dramatically holds back our ability to be resilient and successful. Their research found that there is a direct correlation between lack of recovery and increased incidence of health and safety problems. A lack of recovery whether by disrupting sleep with thoughts of work, or continuous cognitive arousal by watching phones is lost productivity. Anchor and Gielan propose that the key to resilience is trying really hard, then stopping, recovering and then trying again. Thus, accordingly, the more imbalanced we become due to overworking, the more value there is in activities that allow us to return to a state of balance. Hence, Anchor and Gielan argue that if you try to build resilience at work, you need adequate internal and external recovery periods. They acknowledge internal recovery refers to the shorter periods of relaxation that take place in the workday in the form of short scheduled breaks or unscheduled breaks that shift attention or change to other work tasks, when feeling depleted. External recovery refers to actions that take place outside of work – the free time between the workdays, and during weekends, holidays or vacation. They suggest that when the body is out of alignment from overworking, we waste vast mental and physical resources trying to return to balance before we can move forward. Therefore, if you spend too much time in the performance zone you need more time in the recovery zone. Good leaders recognise that you need time to recover and need self-care both for yourself and for those around you. You need to recognise what happens if you do not make time for self-nourishment and recovery. Good leaders will have the compassion to recognise this.

Finding inner calm

Finding your own inner calm may be a way forward for some individuals. Jawad and Kakabadse (2019) believe that resilient people have the capacity and responsibility to determine their own destiny rather than feeling powerless in a specific situation. As such, inner calm is needed to display an external appearance of calm. They propose that high resilience intelligence (RQ) gives the individual the emotional capacity to survive work without falling apart under intense pressure, when in senior roles, which often involve a continual stream of political strife. Accordingly, they believe that resilience is hard and that it requires the courage to confront painful realities, whilst having the faith to believe that there will be a solution when one is not immediately evident. Finding inner calm is part of a personal strategy for resilience, and it forms an inward dive into self to find peace in stormy times.

Summary

Resilience is the ability to work through and survive a distinctly stretching experience as well as having the capacity to face adversities. For this reason, exploring resilience enables us to realise that this is an attribute which is distinctly individual and unique. This involves building up your positive emotions, being aware of contagion and valuing your own bank of positivity. This was a key finding from the research, which supported the views presented on valuing psychological capital. Time for recovery is part of the process of healing and this needs to be acknowledged. Even though resilience is made up of various perspectives it has become a type of intelligence in its own right (RQ) and can also be known as personal resilience, which may be named PRQ. In essence an integral approach is discussed, which supports a holistic overview of personal resilience.

References

Anchor S & Gielan M (2017) *Resilience Is About How You Recharge Not How You Endure*. Cited in *Emotional Intelligence Resilience* (2017), Harvard Business Review Publishing Corporation, Boston, MA

Avey, Luthans & Yousseuf (2010) Cited in Zehira C & Narcıkarab E (2016) Effects of Resilience on Productivity Under Authentic Leadership, Science Direct 12th International Strategic Management Conference, ISMC, 28–30 October, Antalya Turkey. Proceedings in *Social and Behavioral Sciences*, 235, 250–258

Bennis W (2013) Leadership in a Digital World: Embracing Transparency and Adaptive Capacity, *MIS Quarterly*, 37:2, June

Coutu D L (2017) *How Resilience Works Emotional Intelligence Resilience*, Harvard Business School Publishing Corporation, Boston, MA

Fredrickson B L (1998) What Good Are Positive Emotions? *Review of General Psychology: Special Issue: New Directions in Research on Emotion*, 2, 300–319

Fredrickson B L (2001) The Role of Positive Emotions in Positive Psychology: The Broaden-and-Build Theory of Positive Emotions, *American Psychologist: Special Issue*, 56, 218–226

Fredrickson B L (2009) *Positivity: Ground-Breaking Research to Release Your Inner Optimist and Thrive*, Oneworld, Oxford Press, Oxford

Hansen S (2018) *Resilience Enables Strategic Agility*, Global Resilience Report, The Resilience Institute Europe

Jawad A Q & Kakabadse A (2019) *Leadership Intelligence: The 5Qs for Thriving as a Leader*, Bloomsbury Business Publishing, London and New York

Kopans D (2017) *How to Evaluate, Manage and Strengthen Your Resilience.* Cited in *Emotional Intelligence: Resilience Editor* (2017), Harvard Business School Publishing Corporation, Boston, MA

Luthans Youssef et al. (2007) Cited in Zehira C & Narcıkarab E (2016) Effects of Resilience on Productivity Under Authentic Leadership, Science Direct 12th International Strategic Management Conference, ISMC, 28–30 October, Antalya Turkey. Proceedings in *Social and Behavioural Sciences*, 235, 250–258

Morris R (2004) Cited in Neenan M (2018) *Developing Resilience: A Cognitive-Behavioural Approach*, Routledge Taylor & Francis Group, London and New York

Neenan M (2018) *Developing Resilience: A Cognitive-Behavioural Approach*, Routledge Taylor & Francis Group, London and New York

Northouse P G (2018) *Introduction to Leadership: Concepts and Practices*, Sage, Thousand Oaks, CA

Seligman M (2011) *Flourish: A Visionary Understanding of Happiness and Wellbeing*, GB Nicholas Brealey Publishing, London

Sonnenfeld J A & Ward A J (2017) Firing Back: *How Great Leaders Rebound After Career Disasters*, Cited in *Emotional Resilience* (2017) Editor, Harvard Business School Publishing Corporation, Boston, MA

Tugade M M & Fredickson B L (2004) Resilience Individuals Use Positive Emotions to Bounce Back from Negative Emotional Experiences, *Journal of Personality and Social Psychology*, 86:2, 320–333

Young J (2018–2019) *Research Interview Insights on Resilience Study*, The Creative Digital Community, North East, UK. Research first published in this volume

Zehira C & Narcıkarab E (2016) Effects of Resilience on Productivity Under Authentic Leadership, Science Direct 12th International Strategic Management Conference, ISMC, 28–30 October, Antalya Turkey. Proceedings in *Social and Behavioural Sciences*, 235, 250–258

5

SELF-AWARENESS, VISION, VALUES AND SELF-KNOWLEDGE

How well do you know yourself? Leadership will test all your abilities to ride a storm, conquer and be restrained, when met by the highs and lows of the journey. To be a leader you do of course first have to understand yourself! You need to know your own limitations, have self-belief and have confidence in your own decision-making abilities. Knowing who you are, what you stand for and who you want to be is all part of leadership.

Self-awareness

There is no doubt that good leaders need to first understand themselves, before they can lead. This involves a deep understanding of your own emotional self-awareness, level of empathy and personal limitations. "The first essential step in developing resilience is taking personal responsibility for guiding yourself through tough times with all its pain and struggle, trial and error (you can of course seek support along the way)" Neenan

DOI: 10.4324/9780367280970-5

(2018). Appreciating these elements helps create the self-knowledge and self-confidence necessary to make the right decision, know when to bring in extra support and feel confident about what is required to move forward. As such, the innovative leader understands complexity, appreciates resilience, values tacit and intangible knowledge and uses emotional intelligence as a key factor for innovative management. The self-awareness aspect was encountered in this study and is highlighted in the following quotes.

> *"For me, the prime issue about leadership is around understanding and knowing yourself. So, it's about spending enough time thinking about, reflecting upon, trying to understand what you are about. The questions can be in all sorts of forms, whether they be about: What am I here for? What do I want to leave behind in the sense of legacy? What do I want to contribute?"*
>
> Male, experienced Creative Digital Executive Coach

> *"So, what's important in my own entrepreneurial journey? Staying true to myself; working out how to be effective and being relentless in a sort of pursuit of personal development to find out what works and to keep testing, but do so in a way which is ethical and respects other people's boundaries."*
>
> Male Creative Digital Founder

> *"I check in on myself as I am self-aware."*
>
> Male Managing Director

> *"I think I have self-awareness because I do a lot of reflection. So, I think I've learned about myself through that, but we are really complicated. So, I understand myself, fully. I'm not sure that a lot of people I work with do, really."*
>
> Male, experienced Creative Digital Executive Coach

Self-belief is a strong, but not unrealistic, conviction that you can move your life in the direction you want to go but embraces compassionate self-acceptance as a fallible human being (Neenan 2018).

Working on ourselves:

> *"So, firstly, I think leadership starts from within and is basically doing the work on ourselves."*
>
> Male Creative Digital Founder

> *"The whole notion of resilience for me is that we can connect that back to the notion of emptiness or the 'well' being empty or rock-bottom. Because, that notion of resilience is your ability to continue to not give up, to stay in there and some of the issues for me are around resilience . . . one aspect is having a sufficient sense of self that you can cope."*
>
> Male, experienced Creative Digital Executive Coach

Self-awareness is a contributing factor to leadership as you need to understand self and your limitations before you can lead others. As previously mentioned, one leader is checking in with their emotions to check how they feel.

Finding purpose, meaning and passion

Understanding your own purpose and passion helps in achieving meaning from life. As discussed earlier in Chapter 4, Coutu (2017) believes that making decisions that bring meaning and purpose in life supports a tendency for resilience. Neenan (2018) uses a cognitive-behavioural approach and discusses the meaning, attitudes and beliefs that people attach to adverse life events. As such, when we uncover the beliefs and values that we believe in and link this to our professional values in the workplace then deep meaningful work can result. If the work has little personal value and there is a lack of passion, then it will be more difficult to stand firm and become resilient. Out of alignment between personal and professional values, passion and purpose can result in lack of motivation. This focus on finding meaning is also part of the positive psychology criteria as discussed previously by Seligman. Again, this is highlighted by digital leaders interviewed, supported by quotes from this study.

Meaning and identity

> *"Now, it is interesting because I have done some research around people who have fallen into depression and all sorts of other things like that and half the time it is because they've lost their identity; they've lost their meaning. So, if you can almost develop that in people you can pull them out of where they are at. So, for me, in every situation now, if I see it going a little downhill for me it's about, okay, what is the identity; what is the meaning and how can we pull that around."*
>
> Male Managing Director

"I would challenge people who are struggling to really turn their back on themselves and think about what drives you, honestly – and that's not an easy question."

Male Managing Director of a digital company

"For me it comes back to meaning. Things that don't have meaning, then, they don't motivate people into action. So, spend time finding out what you are really about. What's important to you is a precursor to deciding where you're going to work or what you're going to do."

Experienced Creative Digital Executive Coach

"What's important to me on the journey is doing things that align with my deepest personal meaning, my sort of inner teacher; What are my values? What do I actually want to achieve and what brings me to life?"

Male Creative Digital Founder

Purpose and Passion

"Going back to my earlier conversation about purpose – thinking what is this mission that I'm on – what's the contribution, what difference do I want to make? But, wrapped around that has to be what do you deem to be important? What is your value system?"

Experienced Creative Digital Executive Coach

Describing how he found resilience and recovered from a position of rock-bottom, one leader explains how he found his passion and what he truly excelled at, and this helped him to flourish.

"I read this book and took a lot out of it and what it was driving at was about simplicity. It was understanding and being brutally honest with what it is that you and your organisation is actually good at. Effectively understating what your passion is, understanding what you are truly excellent at doing and then finding a business model that allows you to leverage those sorts of things."

"So ultimately passion and confidence and bringing those together. It is not mere confidence; it is also excellence and what you know you are good at. So I understood our passion and understand that we happen to be unusually good at running this type of business."

Male Managing Director of a digital company

The interviewees discussed finding meaning, identity and purpose as part of resilience. Another perspective arising was finding meaning by helping others through their difficulty and pain. As such, these leaders were using empathy and emotional intelligence to help others and at the same time to find purpose and meaning within their own lives.

Flip it – by helping other people

We don't always automatically think of helping others as a way through our own difficulties but this ability to rise to another level and give back and help others possibly takes the mind off the current challenges and adversity whilst using your skill set to help others more in need and, as a result, finding purpose and meaning in life. Thus, taking a broad view of life rather than being insular and self-focused. The following leader discussed helping other people.

> *"I think helping other people is something that is almost a distraction of your own pain and suffering but then it helps you recover, because I think what it does is – you see positivity through other people, and I love helping other people."*
>
> Male Serial Entrepreneur

By helping others, you do indeed help yourself. Therefore, less focus on self and more focus on others is indeed transformational.

Alignment to personal and professional values

Alignment to self (your own values) and matching those values to the organisation you work in, or have created, is key to being in the flow. Edmondson (2019) suggests that if your ideas are not getting a positive reception or you are not learning about your colleagues or organisation that you had expected then that may suggest that you are not in a job that is a good fit with your personal values and goals. If this is the case, you may want to look for new opportunities.

The qualitative interview data significantly highlighted this.

> *"So, what I seek to do is, I seek to embody my values and actually, you know meditate on that so it's within me rather than just what I say. So . . . because, actually, what I've*

> *found in terms of, you know, relationships and experiences, I have found that I fall short. So, what work do I need to do to actually make that change for myself."*
>
> Male Managing Director

> "What people look for is what you say and actually what you do, and do they align, and are they the same? So, the challenge is, how do you gain alignment between what you say and what you do and how does it come from within rather than being just on the surface."
>
> "I think it is also the case that people who I learn whose values are not aligned to mine, I seek to focus my efforts elsewhere. That's also vulnerable because you forego the opportunity to do stuff with people and you have to pay the price for that."
>
> Male Creative Digital Founder

> *"I hear about these values and they just don't connect (to the business)."*
>
> Male Managing Director

These leaders all discuss values but crucially what they are discussing is the connection between what people say and what they do, and that they are observing this behaviour in others. More importantly, being out of alignment with yourself means that you cannot be your authentic self, and this means you are not on track in terms of your own journey, and you may find you are being pulled in a direction that prevents you from living your truth.

Developing emotional intelligence and empathy

For Daniel Goleman (2012) emotional intelligence refers to the capacity for recognizing our own feelings and those of others, for motivating ourselves, and for managing emotions well in ourselves and in our relationships. An influential theorist, Howard Gardener (2006) highlighted the distinction between intellectual and emotional intelligence and proposed a model of multiple intelligence. His list of seven kinds of intelligence included two personal varieties – knowing one's inner world and social adeptness. We now know the personal aspects as emotional intelligence and social intelligence. In 1990 Salovey and Mayer proposed a comprehensive theory of emotional intelligence. They defined emotional intelligence as being able to monitor and regulate one's own and others' feelings, and to use feeling to guide thought and action. In emotional intelligence research, self-awareness is the ability to understand one's own feelings and make an accurate self-assessment (Gardner & Stough 2020). Goleman adapted a model to include five basic emotional and social competences including self-awareness (knowing what we feel to guide decision-making); self-regulation (handling emotions and recovering from distress); motivation (using deepest preferences to guide us towards our goal and persevere in face of setbacks); empathy (sensing what people are feeling and cultivating rapport) and social skills (handling emotions in relationships, cooperation, and teamwork). In this way, emotional competencies can contribute to excellence. Goleman et al. suggests that emotional competencies were twice as important in contributing to excellence as were pure intellect and expertise.

Empathy, as part of emotional intelligence, involves standing in the shoes of another person to appreciate what it is like to be in their shoes. Some people have naturally high levels of empathy; however, empathy is something that can be developed and worked on. Again, whilst some leaders are good at handling their emotions and forming cooperative relations with others, some leaders need to work on handling their emotional outbursts and this is a sign of leadership at its best. A classic study by Boyatzis (1982) of 2,000 managers and executives at 12 different organizations found that of 16 abilities that distinguished accomplished leaders from average performers, all involved emotional intelligence, except for two abilities. According to Goleman, a study by McClelland also highlighted that another ability that distinguished stars from average leaders – was a set of cognitive abilities – pattern recognition and "big-picture" thinking, was 13 percent greater among star leaders.

Applying emotional intelligence in the digital era

The previous section suggests that top leaders should strive to develop their emotional intelligence. Goleman et al. highlights that the single most important factor in job performance and advancement is emotional intelligence. Additionally, in a virtual and hybrid workplace environment this is increasingly becoming a key skill set. Goleman et al. suggest that the premium on emotional intelligence can only rise as organizations become increasingly dependent on the talents and creativity of workers who are independent agents. He goes on to propose that virtual teams can be especially agile because they are headed by whoever has the requisite skills, rather than someone who has the title Manager. Moreover, the human ingredient is key for digital leaders. Within the research a deep understanding of emotional intelligence was not forthcoming. Some leaders talked about emotional stability, but fewer mentioned applying empathy. The good news is that emotional intelligence can be developed.

Leadership and knowingness

As part of your repertoire do you use your own personal knowledge and knowingness to make decisions? Do digital leaders always use a rational approach to making decisions? The traditional management theory suggests that they make decisions after carefully considering a variety of options to choose from based on facts and data. Many leaders do this within – medium and large sized – business. However, the small business founder may take an alternative route. The "serial entrepreneur" in the research discussed how he was constantly guided by "gut feelings" and intuition. In other words, a deep interior knowingness that one taps into to make decisions. In the case of a serial entrepreneur, they have of course already acquired many rich experiences, a type of observed tacit knowledge and lived experience that stands them in good stead. Added to this, their own "inner intuitive knowingness" creates a different type of personal knowledge and knowing. This leader has the ability and confidence to override a "facts-based approach" to decision-making.

Polanyi (1967) introduced the concept of "knowing" and "instinct," and discussed an individual's sensing of deep knowingness, which arises from instinct rather than rational thought. This type of "don't know what we don't know" thinking is part of the core element of what is known as tacit knowledge. Polanyi suggests that we should reconsider human knowledge by starting from the position that we can know more than we can tell. He questions whether we may have a tacit foreknowledge of yet undiscovered things. According to Polanyi we can be aware of hidden implications and look for clues to reality in this inner world. As such, emphasising that in terms of the pursuit of knowledge, we are at all times guided by sensing the presence of a hidden reality towards which clues are pointing. Access to this knowledge is only available if we are prepared to listen to it. This type of know-how is individual and involves reaching down and recognising a level of awareness and consciousness that arises at a very deep level within the individual. According to Polanyi the way we exercise our tacit powers of knowing, suggests that the things that we know in this way include problems and hunches, physiognomies and skills, and the use of tools, probes and an extended list including the primitive knowledge of external objects perceived by our senses. This type of thinking lends itself to Sartre's work on "consciousness and being," which mentions layers of consciousness, available at a deep level in individuals who are awake enough to tap into their "knowing elements." Sartre's thinking suggests that the mind and thinking are external reasoning mechanisms but not necessarily the real "knowing self" which can be listened to and discovered in the interior silence of individuals. Relying on knowingness may therefore be part of tacitness at an individual level. Acting on this knowing can give access to deep realms of personal knowledge.

Decision-making and knowingness

There are two sides to the argument on decision-making in business. The logical side is all about doing the research, creating alternatives and making the final decision based on an evaluation of the options on offer. In addition, there are those who advocate using the latest business analytical tools to make tough decisions. Although, even analytical decision-making tools need some form of interpretation. However, while decisions may need to be made within a broad and overarching context, some daily decisions are made instantly. Many creative leaders believe in using their instinct. Call it gut feel, intuition, insight or knowingness. For the creatives they want to feel it. Does it feel right? They are using that deep "inner knowing" that they carry with them that may have served them well in the past. Of course, it may be necessary to use both sides of the coin (hard and soft) to check out those all-important decisions.

For the digital creative leaders within the interview research the following highlights this phenomenon of applying intuitive tacit knowledge and knowingness:

Sensing

"The knowing suggests that it's cognitive and it's not. 'Sensing' would be a better word [and] having the courage to trust that intuition."

Male, experienced Creative Digital Executive Coach

Gut feeling

"Everything is gut feel, almost, and intuition. Because I know my gut feel is my sort of inner being. So, for me it is a case whereby if my gut feeling is telling me something, I will always listen to it now because the times when I haven't listened it hasn't ended well. I do a sense check to find out what is my gut telling me."

Male Managing Director

Some other leaders give a different perspective promoting the inner voice, instinct, intuition and insight.

Inner voice, instinct and intuition

"I mean, gosh, there's certainly the inner voice that . . . hits the fan! And I have found myself in situations that you simply had not planned for, that life happens. So, life happens, and I then sit and get worried about it, through those natural reactions where you worry about something. You then start to deal with something, and you do whatever you can to put it right or fix it or whatever that is, and whatever is going to happen is going to happen. If you look at 'Well, okay, what's the worst thing that can happen?' Or what is the worst thing that has happened? It is not necessarily . . . you know, going back to your reflective point, it is pointless sitting there worrying about something that has not happened or has happened, is the key thing. So, it is about the here and now, and what can you do now?"

Male Serial Entrepreneur

"Another two key words I think with leaders, which cannot be taught are instinct and intuition. The two words are both my friend and my enemy because when my confidence is up they are my friend, when my confidence is down, they are my enemy because I question myself too much. Almost all the time my gut is right

"The ability of an entrepreneur is to walk around the other side (of the ball) until I have looked all around the ball and I have turned the ball around – the top, the bottom, the dark side, the light . . . All I'm saying is instinct and intuition don't come from nowhere. They come from insight."

Male Creative Digital Entrepreneur

"I would say that part of the journey for me has been developing and understating and trusting intuition. So, having and developing that intuition about where we are and what we are about and a year on we really feel like we've proved that we really can survive."

Male Managing Director of a digital company

When individual leaders have an awareness of the value of their own personal instinctive knowing, this may enable them to make smarter and faster decisions. Despite "knowing and know-how" being a fuzzy area to delve into and define, it lends itself to being a way of living that could encourage transformational change and innovation. For those who are highly "sensory" it is a way of being and living in connection with a higher creative part of themselves. The question is: Can enlightened leadership focused on the development of personal knowing be expanded outward to the collective group level? Senge et al. (2005) highlight the importance of embracing and mobilising "tacit knowledge and knowing" at a collective level within the corporate organisation to transform and encourage deep change and innovation. Young (2012) discusses this in terms of Co-Ka as a form of collective knowledge as part of personal knowledge creation. This is an area for further investigation in the future and brings in elements of group working and collective knowingness as a new way of working.

Summary

In exploring the area of self-awareness – values, passion and purpose support the view of a leader as a Journeyer who delves deeper into their own understanding of self. Moreover, it is important to appreciate that part of the journey involves a continuous cycle of learning that helps to prepare for an environment where finding our route, purpose and identity helps survival in the long term. The Journey person uses all the tools available to them including their own personal knowledge and knowingness. They are aware of emotional intelligence and are prepared to develop this area to understand self and others. This leader knows that resilience is helped when you are in alignment at a deep level with who you are (your authentic self) at every level and when you find purpose and meaning in what you do. For all leader's resilience starts by understanding self.

INDIVIDUAL SELF-ASSESSMENT FOOD FOR THOUGHT

COPING AT THE EDGE
My Story

For me there's a sense of, because I've experienced it personally, before you can be any good to anybody else you have to be good to yourself. That sense of . . . there was a period of my life when I was very much out of sinc with my values. I did not know what it was at the time, but I went through a very difficult 18 months to two years, when I was fine at work because I was busy and making progress but not fine at home. I was not a bad parent or bad father or anything like that, but I was quick to anger, small things annoyed me overly annoyed me and there was clearly something wrong with me. At that time, I was out of sync, but I didn't know what it was that was out, that was wrong with me!

So, I sat down and analysed my life, through simple questions about when have I been happy, when have I been sad; what do I like, what do I dislike? Just to try to get some essence out around what I am about, what is important to me, what is significant.

I had a really strong desire to work for myself and it was just working through that, with having a young family at the time and lots of commitments, saying 'I'd like to do that, but I can't do that.' I was dealing with the frustrations of that disconnect out of syncness.

Coping at the edge:

> *For me, one of the characteristics of where people are getting close to rock-bottom would not be defined as rock-bottom, I would define it as more of 'an edge'; they are on the edge of their ability to cope.*
>
> Discussing a client:
>
> *So, he explained how he was, and I worked with him about what he was experiencing was perfectly natural because of the demands and all the different things he was experiencing in his life; and that we all have limitations about how we cope; but also, how deep our reserves are.*
>
> *This person lost his sense of who he was, and he was in this awful place. Actually, this is a common notion in personal change where we go through a really profound personal development. There is some*

sense of we lost the prior self and it's an awful place, rock-bottom, when the old self has died, and the new self hasn't formed enough yet.

One of the key things with this particular guy, between the old self and the new self, was a shift. Because he went through such a personal trauma of coping with everything, he experienced what trauma is really like. And because he'd experienced what traumas were like, because he was a change agent in the company he worked for, he was then able to understand and appreciate the traumas that other people might experience as he pushed change through the company.

Then of course if you don't (cope) then you are risking really significant ill-health because you're right on the cusp.

Experienced Creative Digital Executive Coach

After reading the personal transformation story, consider the following questions.

1. Does any part of the personal transformation story relate to your own experiences?
2. How often do you use your intuition, or knowingness when making difficult decisions? Is this a skill you have learnt to develop and can trust over time, or are you making decisions from evaluating the options externally only? By reading the personal transformation story what does this tell you about top successful leaders?
3. Do you find yourself being able to be empathetic and stand in the shoes of others? If not, why not? Is this an area of emotional intelligence to be further developed?
4. Have you discovered your own clear set of personal values? What are they and can you list the first five values? Do you live by them?
5. Are you in alignment professionally with your values, passion and purpose? If you are out of alignment what changes might you want to make to truly live your authentic self?
6. Create your own personal vision and write it down.

References

Boyatzis R E (1982) *The Competent Manager: A Model for Effective Performance*, Wiley, New York

Coutu D L (2017) *Emotional Intelligence Resilience*, Harvard Business School Publishing Corporation, Boston, MA

Edmondson A C (2019) *The Fearless Organization: Creating Psychological Safety in the Workplace for Learning, Innovation, and Growth*, John Wiley & Sons, Hoboken, NJ

Gardener H E (2006) *Multiple Intelligences New Horizons in Theory and Practice*, Basic Books, New York

Gardner and Stough Cited in Crawford J A, Dawkins S, Martin A & Lewis G (2020) Putting the leader Back into Authentic Leadership: Reconceptualising and Rethinking Leaders, *Australian Journal of Management*, 45:1, 114–133

Goleman D (2012) *Emotional Intelligence: Why it Can Matter More Than IQ*, Bloomsbury Publishing, London

Masten A S, O'Dougherty M & Wright M (2010) Cited in Neenan M (2018) *Developing Resilience: A Cognitive-Behavioural Approach*, Routledge, Oxon and New York

Neenan M (2018) *Developing Resilience: A Cognitive-Behavioural Approach*, Routledge, Oxon and New York

Salovey P & Mayer J D (1990) Emotional Intelligence, *Imagination, Cognition and Personality*, 9, 185–211

Sartre J P (1976) Cited in Boyle M *Sartre's Circular Dialectic and the Emphasis of Abstract Space*. A History of Space and Place in Ballymum, Dublin. A Paper from the Department of Geography and Sociology, University of Strathclyde

Senge P M, Scharmer C O, Jarawaski J & Flowers B S (2005) *Presence: Exploring Profound Change in People, Organizations, and Society: Human Purpose and the Field of the Future*, Random House Publishing, New York

Polanyi M (1967) *The Tacit Dimension*, Anchor Books, New York

Young J (2012) *Personal Knowledge Capital: The Inner and Outer Path of Knowledge Creation in a Web World*, Chandos/Eslevier, Oxford

Young J (2018–2019) *Qualitative Research Study on Resilience from the Creative Digital* Community, North East, UK. Research first published in this volume

6

CONTEMPORARY STYLES OF LEADERSHIP

Assess Your Style and Create Your Brand!

We all need to understand leadership styles whether we are a corporate executive, manager or budding entrepreneur. It is important to be able to assess your leadership style and determine what is appropriate to use in a variety of circumstances. The world is increasingly becoming more complex with decisions being made at break-neck speed in an increasingly VUCA environment (volatility, uncertainty, complexity and ambiguity). This acronym was originally used by the American military to describe extreme conditions. Because of these conditions, innovative leaders need to evaluate complexity, appreciate resilience, value tacit and intangible knowledge and use emotional intelligence as a key to innovative practice. Questions being asked include: How then do we as managers and leaders respond in this ever changing, complex, ambiguous and digital environment? What styles or brand of leadership do we have to adapt too in order to survive? In the early part of the twenty-first century a proactive approach to learning and creating collaborative, cooperative, flexible and agile conditions in the workplace helps leaders

DOI: 10.4324/9780367280970-6

to ride the tide of change on the journey ahead. In a future that will involve hybrid working, appreciating styles of leadership is crucial.

Leadership styles

Whilst there are hundreds of styles of leadership, this chapter focuses on a number of styles that are currently necessary for survival in a contemporary digital business environment. Leaders need to first understand self before they can lead as discussed in Chapter 5. This involves deep levels of self-awareness including personal limitations. This helps create the self-knowledge necessary to make the right decision within the right context, build confidence, inspire others and know when to add extra support. Leaders can then "walk the talk" by being authentic and creating their own brand, vison and values to fit their personal belief system.

Transactional and transformational leadership styles

Most leaders want to be in the transformational leadership camp, but many still find themselves operating from a transactional leadership style. Transactional leadership deals with leaders and followers based on their transactions and is a directive style that manages day-to-day activity, relying heavily on formal power and position. The problems with transactional leaders are that they motivate and reward people with carrots and punish them with sticks! This style lacks consideration for people's ideas, needs and feelings as it focuses on planning, organizing, directing and controlling through manipulation and reward. It does not develop people to their fullest potential or contribution. This is a very traditional control-orientated style portrayed by contingent reward and only really appeals to those who are driven by financial reward rather than through deep and meaningful consideration. The antithesis is transformational leadership where leaders achieve performance that is above and beyond normal – through consideration of individual staff – with a focus on raising motivation and future possibilities to new heights and as a result, changing how people feel about themselves. Transformational leaders inspire and motivate those around them.

The knowledge leader

Knowledge leaders create an organisation filtered through the Company's identity, culture and existing management systems. An obstacle is the leaders' "way of seeing the world." Cavaleri et al. (2005) from a knowledge and leadership perspective ask questions such as: Why do some leaders focus on exercising control over employees, while others focus on liberating their creativity? Why do some leaders view employees as costly whilst others see them as a source of innovation and profitability?

Introducing the yogi

Steven Cavaleri discovered a very interesting book in 1945 in a bookshop in Warsaw, Poland, entitled *The Yogi and the Commissar* by Arthur Koester (1945). When Cavaleri read Koester's work he found that Koester used *The Yogi and the Commissar* to represent two divergent leadership world views. Koester had created a dichotomy to reflect the two strikingly different philosophies. Cavaleri et al. (2005) share Koester's original story and the main arch-types. In this work, the commissar emphasises structuralism, or structured work that starts with concrete mechanics such as organisational charts, rules, procedures and systems. The commissar moulds people's behaviour and believes the structure of a system governs the behaviour of those who work within it. Therefore, if you break the rules you must be controlled and removed from promotion, assigned unfavourable work or dismissed. These are all powerful incentives for making sure people comply. On the other hand, the yogi takes a humanism approach to organisational development and change, believing that there are no quick fixes to problems or easy ways to win people to your side. The yogi believes natural change occurs when people have natural incentives to make changes, and, as such, argues that structuralism as applied by a commissar leads to compliance but not commitment. The yogi wants to give workers the opportunity to express their feelings and engage in dialogue with management to arrive at a shared vision. For the yogi, peak performance is all about enthusiastic members working together as a team with a shared vision.

Focusing on these two-extreme arch-types enables us to immediately capture the stark contrast between the two approaches. As we know today, the old order still exists, and the commissar often unexpectedly appears. The concept is a powerful reminder of two contrasting leadership archetypes. The yogi represents an attractive resonant leadership style that when applied may fit with the creation of an innovative and collaborate culture, whilst the commissar is undoubtedly in the disfavourable dissonant category as discussed within primal leadership (Goleman et al. 2013). The yogi as a style of leadership, as previously illustrated, forms part of the concept of a leader as a Sage (Fig 11.2). This is a powerful metaphor for the age that we live in, where the Sage uses soft skills to stay calm in a storm.

Wisdom leadership

Taking an innovative perspective, Nonaka and Takeuchi (2011) argue that business now demands a different kind of leader – one who will make decisions knowing that the outcomes must be good for society as well as for the company. Hence, they suggest leaders must keep a higher purpose in mind. From this perspective, practical wisdom is tacit knowledge acquired from experience that enables people to make prudent judgements and take actions based on the actual situation, guided by values and morals. They argue that when leaders cultivate such knowledge through an organization, they will be able not only to create knowledge but also to make enlightened decisions. Nonaka and Takeuchi (2011) introduce the phrenetic leader who makes judgments and takes actions amid constant flux. Their research shows that to lead in this way, the following abilities are essential for wise leaders: judge goodness, grasp the essence, create shared context, and communicate the essence so everyone can understand it to foster practical wisdom in others. The phrenetic leader is a type of wisdom leader much like the yogi.

Situational leadership "plug and play"

If you were playing golf on the golf course, it would be imperative to choose the right golf club according to need. This would entail diagnosing the need according to the task or situation you find yourself within. In leadership terms diagnosing a situation has come to be known as "situational leadership" (Hersey & Blanchard 2012). The emphasis here is on thinking before you act, by determining the level of the follower's task maturity or psychological maturity. Situational leaders think about the situation and task of the staff and choose the appropriate leadership style according to the diagnosed situation. Hersey and Blanchard proposed four styles for situational leadership based on the competence of staff (high relationship and low task, high task and high relationship, low relationship and low task and high task and low relationship). This may involve a directing style, where the leader provides specific direction and closely monitors tasks and accomplishments; a coaching style of facilitation; supporting, where the leaders are highly directive and supportive; delegating, which is low on support and on directive behaviour; and a directing style that is high on directive and low on supportive behaviour. Hersey and Blanchard believe in different strokes for different folks! Moreover, situational leaders learn to demonstrate four core, common and critical leadership competencies: diagnose, adapt, communicate and advance. To diagnose involves understanding the situation one is trying to influence; to adapt is to adjust behaviour in response to the contingences of the situation; then communicate by interacting with others in a manner they can understand and accept; and advance by managing the movement. This is a powerful concept to appreciate and supports the leader's ability to diagnose and analyse the task and situation before choosing the style (plug and play) as appropriate.

Primal or resonant leadership (with emotional intelligence) – plug and play

It is the famous writers of emotional intelligence who set the scene in terms of creating primal leadership (also known as resonant leadership), that is heavily based on research (Goleman et al. 2013, 2002). The authors demonstrate attractive, positive, resonant styles of leadership and call attention to more repellent dissonant styles. Goleman et al. like Hersey & Blanchard present six rather than four types of leadership – visionary, coach, democrat, affiliate, pacesetter and commander. The first four styles listed are the positive resonant attractors, whilst the last two styles, pacesetting and commanding, are repellent and dissonant. It is necessary to appreciate that a commanding and dissonant position is appropriate on occasions, when there is imminent danger (such as lives at risk). However, using this style consistently over time will be deeply offensive and repellent. The same is true of a pacing style, a style where pressure is exerted on staff to quickly finish projects. Although this may be appropriate on occasions, for a high-pressured deadline, it should not be seen as a permanent style used regularly, because it leads to burnout and high staff turnover. Less benign and clueless leaders use rigid commanding and pace-setting styles that may prevent people telling the truth. Such a leader may create silence at a high cost (Goleman et al. 2002). In a contemporary environment, it is important to appreciate the impact that the chosen style of leadership will have on staff motivation. Primal leadership is hugely important as it signals what type of leadership is attractive and what is negative. Primal leadership strategy with its focus on applying emotional intelligence, empathy and intentional change and highlighting resonant and dissonant styles, enables the leader to assess the impact of their style of leadership, and by doing so make a decision about the type of culture they will create. Primal leadership means using emotional intelligence and empathy in a positive manner to create positive cultures and work environments that followers are attracted too.

The servant leader

It may be that you see yourself as a servant leader. A leadership theory that has been linked to ethics, virtues and morality is servant leadership (Parris & Peachy 2013). It was Greenleaf and Spears (1970; 1977; 2002) who first introduced the concept of the servant leader. As a viable leadership theory, it provides the ethical grounding and leadership framework needed to help address the challenges of the twenty-first century (Parris & Peachy 2013). Spears (1998) identifies ten characteristics of a servant leader: listening, empathy, healing, awareness, persuasion, conceptualisation, foresight, stewardship, nurturing personal growth and building community. However, Parris & Peachy focus on service to others and they suggest that servant leaders recognise that the role of the organisation is to create people who can build a better tomorrow. This approach resonates with both scholars and practitioners who are responding to the growing perception that corporate leaders have become selfish, and to those who are in fact seeking a viable leadership theory to help resolve present-day challenges. Moreover, it is Greenleaf's earlier conceptualisation of servant leadership as a way of life, rather than a management technique, that stands out. The following story from the research interviews illustrates one entrepreneur's experience of servant leadership.

MOVING INTO TECHNOLOGY-BASED ENTREPRENEURSHIP AND RECEIVING SUPPORT AND AUTONOMY

I got headhunted by various companies. However, one Head/CEO flew into the airport from the USA to see me. For somebody to take that time out to see me in the UK was inspiring. He inspired me by the actions. Actions speak louder than words. When I finally went to work in America that is what I instigated – 'we have to give time for each other.'

Further on in the journey in the United States, I met a survivor in the group and he had been with the company a long time. He was older, and I was this young dynamic guy. Whilst in America he took the time to integrate me into the company. He went out of his way to invite me to dinner. He did not have to do that. Words of wisdom did come through! I learnt he was not a survivor – he was a smart cookie! It is all about treating people as people, for me, coming from working in the past for a hard-nosed Swiss company.

He always had time by being himself and survived in that culture. That was a massive learning curve. He was always there to say: 'I am here to support you' and encouraged high-level responsibility. That was the first big lesson in leadership – 'I am just here to support you' and that was fine. It was servant leadership almost. Nothing wrong in being in a hierarchy, but that means nothing. I see plenty of people who can influence from where they are as hierarchical positions mean nothing. It comes down to individuals. But . . . you can influence from anywhere. You have to be the leader you are – not what someone else wants you to be! I learnt to be the leader I am – I have to be the leader I want to be, because if I am not happy, I am not motivated.

Male Managing Director

This interviewee's story exemplifies learning by example from leaders who inspire us. Some points in the quote overlap into authentic leadership as discussed next. The strength of servant leadership is in encouraging followers through learning, growth and autonomy (Bass 2000). Many entrepreneurs do see themselves as servant leaders as they build and grow the business in size and take responsibility for their employees. Moreover, this style of leadership adds a moral ethical dimension and suggests putting others and society first, for this reason, responsibility, ethics and service, are the key themes in this approach.

The authentic leader

The authentic leader adds yet another dimension to the styles of leadership discussed so far. Authenticity is a way of being and operating in alignment with your true self and is regarded as a pillar of positive organisational scholarship. The demand for authentic and more accountable leaders has encouraged the development of theories based on a leader's moral character. Leading writers include Bill George and Marshall Goldsmith who have both fully developed their own concept of authentic leadership. Bill George's famous book *Discover Your True North* is about leaders aligning to their truth and full potential. In other words, understanding who you are, what your values and purpose are and making sure you align your personal and professional self to your higher purpose (true north). George (2003, 2008) proposes five dimensions that the authentic leader needs to develop. This consists of purpose and passion; values and behaviour; heart and compassion; relationships and connectedness; and self-discipline and consistency. In particular, George believes that understanding values leads to a set of behaviours: building relationships leads to connectedness, self-discipline leads to consistency, living with heart leads to compassion whilst understanding your purpose leads to passion. Moreover, authentic leaders have a desire to serve, empower others, build enduring relationships, develop consistent self-discipline and develop self through personal growth. This spectrum encourages living in alignment with the authentic person that you really are, and this is powerful, as people see beneath the veneer of a fake leader/faux self (Goleman et al. 2013). This style of leadership involves tapping into and being true to your values, not your ego, connecting with others through your heart not your persona and living your life with discipline. George highlights that passion for your purpose comes when you are highly motivated and believe in the intrinsic value of your worth by using your abilities to maximum effect. He goes on to say that having found the purpose that ignites your passion, you then have to test your values in the crucible of life's experiences. George emphasises that you may need to find a company where there is a solid fit between your own values and the organisation's value. Truth North is finding your own compass based on your passion and values and leading with this in mind. This style of leadership draws upon empathy and emotional intelligence as well as self-awareness. Therefore, there are overlaps with both primal leadership and servant leadership within this theory. Authenticity becomes a way of life. Quotes from the interview data highlight these points.

Passion and authenticity

"How can you bring your passion, your authenticity and your genuineness to something and then, if other people want to call that leadership, that's fine. But, actually, it's incredibly dangerous, risk-taking, basically, sometimes that often comes back to bite you but it's about living your beliefs. So, that's much more embodied leadership rather than just stuff that you're coached to do because it comes from within and it's about courage."

Male Leader

Taking the mask off!

"And it is not a mask now, it used to be a mask. It used to be where inside I was churning away but outside, I'd be straight faced."

Male Managing Director

George (2003) goes on to propose that although we may be born with leadership potential, all of us have to develop this ourselves. The way to develop into an authentic leader is not to focus on the destination but the journey itself – a journey to find your true self and the purpose of your life's work. He believes the journey is a never-ending process and takes many years to refine but that the journey is rewarding and fulfilling. Authentic leadership development is a strategy that has also been positioned as an antidote to unethical leadership behaviours (Crawford et al. 2020). Authentic leadership is based on a leader's moral character, integrity, and the consistency between principles, words and actions. Beddoes-Jones and Swailes (2015) in their empirical qualitative study of leaders produced three pillars of authentic leadership. A first pillar of self-awareness: relationships, strengths, weakness, empathy, influence and impact. A second pillar of ethics: integrity, honour, courage, honesty, transparency and fairness, and the third pillar comprised self-regulation: discipline, energy, flexibility, emotional control, patience and resilience. The three pillars are underpinned with a trust infrastructure that leads to relationship building. The overlap between authentic leadership and self-awareness in leadership and emotional intelligence and ethics has already been strongly emphasised in this study. The authentic leadership model on its own is not enough, as leaders need to understand their own personal philosophy of leadership and how that relates to the wider leadership literature to be truly effective (Cunliffe 2009). Authentic leadership is a powerful style of leadership that fits well with the challenges ahead in a fast-moving digital environment.

The leader as a coach

Coaching is a style of leadership and a facilitative process to bring the best out in others. It forms part of the soft skills that leaders can acquire and has a positive impact on staff performance. It is about getting the best out of other people. The coach must think of their people in terms of their potential not their performance (Whitemore 2009). Whitemore believes that underlying the ever-present goal of coaching is building up the self-belief of others, regardless of the content of the task or issue. The leader as a coach explores and encourages the potential of their coachee. Whitemore proposes that coaching is a way of managing and treating people, a way of thinking, and a way of being.

Compared to other styles of leadership the coach believes that the coachees themselves have all the answers. The coaching style is open and the leader as a coach gently explores and questions the coachee to uncover their views. The coach does not give them the answer but facilitates a process of questioning to elicit options and solutions. The benefit of using coaching questions, rather than giving advice, is that questions hold the power to cause others to think, create credible answers and motivates them to act on those ideas. Questioning moves beyond passive acceptance of what others say – or staying stuck in present circumstances – to enable the coachee to creatively solve problems (Stoltzfus 2008).

A quote from the research interviews suggests that you coach to allow people to go on a journey.

> *"The heart of coaching is that you don't tell anyone anything; but rather you allow people to go on the journey!"*
>
> Male Leader

Peterson and Hicks (1994) describe coaching as the "process of equipping people with the tools, knowledge and opportunities they need to develop themselves and become more successful." The authors believe that good coaches orchestrate rather than dictate development. In other words, coaches are like the director of an orchestra who conducts the musicians and artists around him. Peterson and Hicks believe good coaches help followers clarify career goals, identify and prioritize development needs, create and agree to development plans, and create environments that support learning and coaching. Moreover, Hughes et al. (2019) recommend that when leaders coach, they forge a relationship and build a development plan that outlines the actions the coachee will take. They note that leaders need to spend time listening to the coachee to understand the coachee's career aspirations, values, intrinsic motivators, view of the organisation and current work situation. Good leaders are eager to use this process and develop their facilitation and listening skills to encourage staff to move forward in a dynamic way.

A plug for coaching arises from the interview data.

A PLUG FOR COACHING

Just a little plug for coaching. If you do have a coaching-based leadership style then you'd be having maybe five or six conversations a day with people around you. And they would all be reflective conversations. Each time you would be saying, 'okay, what were you trying to achieve here; what did you try out; what worked; what other ideas have you got?' All of that would be reflective. You don't have to take two hours to do that, you can do that in 10–15 minutes.

And not only then are you doing that and having those conversations but you're encouraging that way of thinking in the individual as well. If you've done that five or six times, the individual is then going to think, 'I'm going to have a chat with —; better have some ideas put together here because that's what she's going to ask me about. So, I might as well come along prepared.' So, then, it gets embedded in the way of thinking for everybody inside the organisation.

Male International Coach and Consultant

The victim and rescuer

"So, in transactional analysis there's a concept called the drama triangle invented by Dr Steven Karpman. So, he talks about these three points of the triangle. He talks about a victim, the rescuer and, I guess, the thing that is oppressing you. So, oftentimes, people assume the role of a rescuer to help other people. So, it's actually how do we reframe that so that what happens is that instead of people trying to rescue you – you guide them to coach you so that they help you create your own power rather than them always being one up because they're rescuing you and not taking the power from you rather than actually creating it within you."

Male Leader

The leader makes a powerful point about coaching in a positive way to empower and guide the coachee into the future, rather than rescue them. The leader as a coach would do well to appreciate that rescuing is not appropriate as the role of the coach is to enable, support and empower the coachee.

Models for coaching

Many coaching tools are on offer including the GROW model a metaphor used to explore four areas of (1) goals, (2) reality, (3) options and (4) will, in that order (Whitemore 2009). It is one of the most well-used models of coaching. Another model includes "Sailing the 7C's" by Grimley (2013). Grimley's model fits in with the metaphor of people undertaking a journey and the seven C's are clarity, climate, capability, congruency, confidence, commitment and communication, and framed within C for courage. Whilst, Rogers (2016) coaching model addresses six principles, including: the client is resourceful; the coach's role is to help the client to develop the resourcefulness; coaching addresses the whole person; the client sets the agenda; the coach and client are equal; and coaching is about change and action. Rogers believes that the core purpose of coaching is to increase self-awareness, make choices and to close the gap between what the client is experiencing and what the client is capable of doing. Apart from the famous models of coaching, other models include the ACHIEVE Model by Dembkowski and Eldridge (2003) and LASER by Lee (2003) plus the POSITIVE model by Vincenzo Libri (2004). The skill of coaching can be learnt and developed and elements of each of these models mentioned have something to offer. Coaching is a powerful tool that is transformational for those involved because the coach challenges and teases the answers from the coachee, so that it is the coachee who makes the decision themselves.

Summary

Today's leaders are operating in turbulent times. Evaluating suitable styles of leadership in advance helps anchor the budding leader to gain confidence. Moreover, exploring, appreciating and understanding what styles attract and what styles repel is imperative. Part of this process is to encourage you to assess your own style to create your own brand of leadership for a future that will align with your personal and professional values and ethics. Understanding the styles that produce a positive response is vital and helps create a personal brand with the aim of creating a conducive culture that creates energy and vitality, rather than burn-out, unhappy employees and toxic environments. In this chapter we have discussed various leadership styles that may be helpful including the leader as a yogi, the situational leader, the resonant leader, the servant leader, the authentic leader and the leader as a coach. It is crucial to appreciate the power of the resonant, emotionally intelligent, authentic and calm deeply knowing leader. In a world of hybrid working understanding styles of leadership will still be relevant. Moreover, it is more important than ever to appreciate the need for authentic leadership, servant leadership and coaching, as traditional command and control styles evaporate to be replaced by the evolution of new ways of working and learning in virtual teams as discussed in Chapter 3. The model in Figure 11.2 incorporates some of the styles mentioned in this chapter and aims to present an array of leadership facets required for collaborative working practices suitable for a contemporary digital context.

EXERCISE: TRY USING THE GROW COACHING MODEL

(**GROW = G:** goals and aspirations; **R:** current situation, internal and external obstacles; **O:** possibilities, strengths and resources; **W:** actions and accountability)

Coaching with the **Grow model** might include asking the following questions:

Goals: What is it you are trying to achieve?

Reality: Where are you now? How would you like it to be? What is going on at the moment?

Options: What approaches have you tried so far? What has worked better or worse? Explore the problem (not the solution). What alternatives are there? Is there another way?

Way forward and commitment: What will you do to take this forward? Are you committed? What does commitment look like?

References

Bass B M (2000) The Future of Leadership in Learning Organizations, *The Journal of Leadership Studies*, 7:3, 18–40

Beddoes-Jones F & Swailes S (2015) Authentic Leadership: Development of a New Three Pillar Model, *Strategic HR Review*, 14:3, 94–99

Cavaleri S, Seivert S & Lee W L (2005) *Knowledge & Leadership: The Art and Science of the Knowledge-based Organisation*, Elsevier Butterworth-Heinemann, Oxford

Crawford J A, Dawkins S, Martin A & Lewis G (2020) Putting the Leader Back into Authentic Leadership: Reconceptualising and Rethinking Leaders, *Australian Journal of Management*, 45:1, 114–133

Cunliffe (2009) Cited in Beddoes-Jones F & Swailes S (2015) Authentic Leadership: Development of a New Three Pillar Model, *Strategic HR Review*, 14:3, 94–99

Dembkowski S & Eldridge F (2003) Beyond GROW: A New Coaching Model, *The International Journal of Mentoring and Coaching*, 1:1, November

George B (2003) *Authentic Leadership: Rediscovering the Secrets to Creating Lasting Value*, Jossey-Bass, Wiley Imprint, San Francisco

George B (2008, 2015) *Discover Your True North*, John Wiley Publishers, Toronto, ON

Goleman D, Boyatzis R & McKee A (2002) *The New Leaders: Transforming the Art of Leadership into the Science of Results*, Harvard Business Press, Boston, MA

Goleman D, Boyatzis R E & McKee A (2013) *Primal Leadership: Unleashing the Power of Emotional Intelligence*, Harvard Business Press, Boston, MA

Greenleaf K R & Spears L C (1970; 1977; 2002) *Servant Leadership: A Journey into the Nature of Legitimate Power and Greatness*, Paulist Press, New York

Grimley B Cited in Heather Moyes (Project Manager) (2013) Theory and Practice of NLP Coaching, Perspectives, *Policy and Practice in Higher Education*, 17:4, 148–149

Hersey P & Blanchard K H (2012) *Management of Organizational Behaviour*, FT Publishing

Hughes R L, Ginnett R C Curphy J (2019) *Leadership: Enhancing the Lessons of Experience*, Ninth Edition, McGraw Hill Education, New York

Koester A (1945) Cited in Cavaleri S, Seivert S & Lee W L (2005) *Knowledge & Leadership: The Art and Science of the Knowledge-Based Organisation*, Routledge, London

Lee G (2003) *Leadership Coaching: From Personal Insight to Organisational Performance*, CIPD, London

Libri V (2004) Beyond GROW: In Search of Acronyms and Coaching Models, *The International Journal of Mentoring and Coaching*, 2:1, July

Nonaka I & Takeuchi H (2011) The Wise Leader: How CEO's Can Learn Practical Wisdom to Help Them Do What Is Right for Their Companies, *Harvard Business Review*, 89:5, May

Parris D L & Peachy J W (2013) A Systematic Literature Review of Servant Leadership Theory on Organizational Contexts, *Journal of Business Ethics*, 113, 377–393

Peterson D B & Hicks M D (1994) *Leader as a Coach: Strategies for Coaching and Developing Other*, Personnel Decisions, Minneapolis, MN

Rogers J Fourth Edition (2016) *Coaching Skills: The Definitive Guide to Being a Coach*, McGraw-Hill Publishers, New York

Spears (1998) Cited in Parris D L & Peachey J W (2013) Systematic Literature Review of Servant Leadership Theory on Organizational Contexts, *Journal of Business Ethics*, 113, 377–393

Stoltzfus T (2008) *Coaching Questions: A Coach's Guide to Powerful Asking Skills*, Coach 22 Virgina Beach

Whitemore J (2009) *Coaching for Performance: Growing Human Potential and Purpose. The Principles and Practice of Coaching and Leadership*, Nicholas Brearley Publishing, London and Boston

Young J (2018–2019) *Research Interview Insights from Leadership and Resilience Study*, The Creative Digital Community, North East, UK. Research first published in this volume

7

CONVERSATION AND KINDNESS IN LEADERSHIP

The opposite of isolation is talking! Talking is an external activity that can be developed and worked on with friends, colleagues and coaches. Engaging in conversation and dialogue supports your ability to change and adapt your mental models of the world. The assumptions that you make about yourself and others can be challenged and developed, and your own limiting beliefs may be shaped as you talk through the consequences of a decision. Conversation and dialogue become a powerful communication tool that enables you to reach out to find answers, rather than become isolated and insular.

Conversational leadership

Conversational leadership is part of a knowledge-focused strategy on the leadership agenda. April (1999) emphasises that one only has to go back to Socrates, 2,400 years ago, and his use of conversation as a method for seeking deeper understanding, as way of seeking the rock bottom truth in what

DOI: 10.4324/9780367280970-7

was being discussed. Socrates taught Western Civilisation the art of asking questions as a tool for discovering reality, and for Socrates, "the unexamined life was not worth living." By conversation and dialogue, one begins to make sense of the things we may not previously have talked about, allowing us time to reshape inbuilt assumptions. Most recently, conversational leadership has been spotlighted by David Gurteen's work (2021) as part of knowledge and leadership in contemporary organisations with its particular focus on the importance of knowledge café's for conversation and dialogue. Gurteen underscores that in seeing the world we are not objective, dispassionate observers because we see things through different lens with different filters and in different shapes and forms by years of differing experiences. Conversation opens up the ability to reshape thoughts through dialogue and as such may transform our thinking. In the research, the following leader discusses the importance of a conversational style of leadership in business. A quote from the leadership interviews highlighted the following.

> *"In general terms, I think the most effective way is to base leadership around dialogue and understanding, a conversationally based style. And the more you get that right the less the likelihood is that you are going to have to step in and tell people what to do. I find when I'm talking to a lot of leaders and managers it's the opposite way round. Their natural approach veers towards instructing people, to being prescriptive. That, for me, increases the chance of things going wrong. Then, they use that as justification for being more prescriptive in those scenarios."*
>
> Male International Coach and Consultant

Valuing conversation and dialogue as part of an approach to resilience needs to be part of any leader's agenda.

Reaching out – opening up and connecting

The research confirmed that a key to resilience was the ability to forge relationships and reach out to trusted others. Resilience is not developed in total isolation. A message within the research was "If you know that someone could provide valuable advice in your time of need, seek it." Such support and advice can significantly reduce the duration of your struggle to overcome your problems. Therefore, a balanced view of self-reliance includes both self - and social support (Neenan 2018). The research revealed that this came in the shape and form of reaching out to trusted family and friends in an informal capacity or to members of the Board or other professionals. Additionally, formal methods were also used such as having a coach or mentor where confidentiality could be guaranteed. Some leaders openly said they had a whole network around them that they used on a regular basis. The key was reaching out to trusted "critical friends" who would be able to critique and offer constructive feedback. These frank exchanges that took place were very often in informal settings such as pubs and bars in the city. For some leaders reaching out was a struggle – possibly due to their high status in the community. However, significantly, none of these issues were discussed within the female research sample. The key to conversational learning is to feel safe enough to open-up about issues and challenges showing vulnerability and as such the strength of the relationship itself is crucial.

Reaching out

> *"I feel like I have understood that being able to appreciate that those who are more quiet and less dramatic actually add a lot of value to your life. So reaching out . . . the first step of reaching out is actually understanding who to reach out too – right? . . . Yes, and what is interesting is a lot of those folks are very, typically speaking, are much more value driven than they are transactionally driven."*
>
> Managing Director of a Digital Company

Reframing and examining thinking

Being a flexible thinker (or helping to develop such a mindset), rather than being locked in a fixed viewpoint allows for adaptation to changing circumstances. Neenan (2018) points out that our thinking powerfully influences our feelings and action is the basis of cognitive behavioural therapy (CBT) approach. He suggests that examining our thinking provides an entry point into our inner world enabling us to discover whether our attitudes are helping, hindering or harming us in our struggle to deal with difficult times. It is easy to moderate the intensity of your negative feelings by first modifying the thinking and changing the unproductive behaviour that drives these feelings (Neenan 2018). CBT focuses on uncovering the origins of this problem.

Quotes from the creative digital leaders in this study support Neenan's view.

Honest communication

"I do my best to change my own self-talk."

Male Leader

"To be open to attack. This means to be willing to have your views, opinions, beliefs and assumptions challenged by people, especially when it becomes important to how you rise in an organisation because people will tend to put you on a pinnacle because of authority. People will naturally be cautious and our job as leader is to give courage, to encourage people to be willing to be enthusiastic about telling us what they really think. Absolutely honest communication."

Male, experienced Creative Digital Executive Coach

"It's amazing how stress can come out. I have had ultrasound scans, I have had a chest x-ray, I've been in hospital; just stress; nothing wrong whatsoever. But, when you get that little doubt in your mind you convince yourself that you've got cancer and you are convinced that you're going to die. It escalates. The ball rolls higher. So, understanding yourself, and sometimes I say to myself 'I am fine; you're doing it again."

Male Digital Founder

Vulnerability and emotions

Expressing your vulnerability is a sign of strength in leadership. Neenan (2018) argues that you might see help from others as a sign of weakness. He suggests that resilience is not developed in total isolation and that if you know that someone could provide valuable advice in your time of need, seek it because support and advice can significantly reduce the duration of your struggle to overcome your problems. The work of Brene Brown (2015) focuses on emotions and showing vulnerability. Vulnerability links to trust, because most of us want to be vulnerable around "trusted individuals," and this was validated when leaders talked about reaching out to trusted others in this research study. This means identifying those trusted within your circle.

Learning how to build trust and forming positive relationship is the foundation for building good relationships. Brown believes that if you think about connection on one continuum/anchor, at one end of that continuum is empathy and at the other end of the continuum is shame. It unravels our relationships and our connections with other people, as empathy is about being vulnerable with people in their own vulnerability. Brown defines shame as "the intensely painful feeling or experience of believing that we are flawed and therefore unworthy of love and belonging" she notes that "empathy is the antidote to shame." Brown believes you cannot selectively numb emotions. Leaders cannot ignore both their own emotions or those around them as emotions are literally contagious – we sense and absorb them. Brown believes that we are even more sensitive to the emotions of leaders and others we view as high status. Brown's work takes us to the core of opening-up to others. A quote from Brown's work includes, "So, to fully experience positive emotions, we have to be open to our negative emotions. We have to resist the urge to numb ourselves and cultivate the ability to be vulnerable without feeling compelled to protect ourselves. We have to develop a sense of comfort with our discomfort" (Brown 2012). It is vital for leaders to understand the power of connection and relationship building. Building relationships built on trust and understanding the powerful influence that empathy, positivity and authenticity contribute is important. Additionally, deep listening is also part of this process. It is not always easy to show your vulnerability, but this is a powerful practice and links deeply to being real and authentic. Vulnerability relates to authenticity because you cannot bluff and be authentic at the same time.

The following research quotes from this study's interviews fit with Browns work on vulnerability.

Vulnerability

"Now people who are resilient will tend to have, I propose, wider and greater experiences than people who are not resilient because people who are not resilient, will, by definition, restrain themselves, hold themselves back and will not expose themselves too much. So, for me, part of that notion of resilience links through strongly with the notion of vulnerability."

"What's vulnerability? Vulnerability is our willingness to put ourselves out there and believe that we will cope and survive, which is very similar to some notions of resilience. But for me, if you're going to be a great leader, you have to have the ability to be vulnerable; to be up to attack."

"So, the best leaders, for me, have strength. If we take vulnerability, the willingness to be attacked as well as – one end of the spectrum – and also the willingness to attack – in the sense of the willingness to question or challenge but not attack. Attack is the wrong term in some sense because for me there always has to be a notion of good intention. If we always act out of a premise of good intention, we can tell people what we think they need to know because we are doing it with the intention that it will be helpful. You might not like it."

"The notion of attack is like when someone's attacking it's the ability to stand your ground or have the right arguments or communicate back. That is not always easy to be able to turn that round and send it back. I think that's a skillset."

Male, experienced Creative Digital Executive Coach

For many people opening up, being vulnerable and learning to let go does not come easy. In fact, the interview research underscored that leaders needed to get comfortable with vulnerability as part of a learning journey.

Get comfortable with vulnerability and let go!

"Yes, I mean again the exact words I would use is being comfortable with your vulnerability and accepting it as part of life. The reason you're right to bring this up is, I ran the business as a 90% shareholder . . . one of the many things that happened 365 days a year for 14 years – was the one day I remember letting go. I suppose. Of course, it was alright."

"It was not easy to let go because it was learned behaviour."

Male Creative Digital Entrepreneur

Holding space for vulnerability

"So, it's actually, how do we hold space for that vulnerability? What do we do? How do we do it for ourselves when we do something which is inimical to our own values and how do we pick ourselves up when what we come to realise is that, actually, what we're creating is greater destruction than what we hoped to create?"

"So, how do we hold space for that pain and then how do we find people to work with who can also hold space for us so we can process it and we can actually use it for learning rather than just self-destruction?"

Male Leader

Vulnerability is part of the process of opening up, but as stated it needs to take place with personal and profession colleagues that you can trust and respect.

Kindness and compassion in leadership

No one forgets an act of kindness. Kindness makes a real impact! An act of kindness shows action and behaviour by leading from the front. One aspect of emotional intelligence is compassion and compassion is made up of various aspects of kindness. Kindness is a virtue and a value and can be incorporated into personal and organisational values. Kindness is value-based leadership and is required more than ever in the complex, digital unpredictable turmoil that we find ourselves in. Too little attention has been paid to kindness by leaders, but this is beginning to change as more focus is being paid to this aspect of management. Today, kindness is back on the agenda, but although some work is published in this area it is still an area where more attention and research is required.

Looking back in history we find philosophers in Indian and Chinese culture expound the notion of kindness as part of leadership. Confucius based his philosophy on two ethical premises Li and Yi. Where Li refers to ethical judgements (doing the right thing at the right time, whilst at the same time being pragmatic), Yi refers to reciprocity and doing the right thing for the right reason whilst working towards the greater good. The final focus is on Ren that contains five core values that are seriousness, generosity, sincerity, diligence and kindness. All of which seem most relevant today as we swim in the chaos around us in what is an interconnected, digital and mobile world. Today society is looking for ever deeper meaning when prospects are bleak and inspiration lacking. In the Western world we appear to be focussed on competitive individualism, freedom and independence rather than on collectivism. In a world where leaders may abuse their authority, one argument emphasising kindness in the context of leadership is that it moderates the excess of authority (Mayer 2017). It is all too easy for leaders to abuse their authority to the detriment of sub-ordinates.

In our society, Haskins (2018) points out that competitiveness abounds and winning or finding winners easily becomes an excuse for not being kind. It makes sense that the world, organisations and society would be kinder as long as kindness is pursued for altruistic purposes and not for self-gain or aggrandisement. Haskins suggests that kindness in leadership includes the impact on employees, teams, management, culture, reputation, performance, customers and business partners. She suggests the reputational impact includes an ability to attract and retain both customers and the most talented employees, while the performance impact is shown in reduced transaction costs. She goes on to state that the evidence obtained is anecdotal. However, by applying kindness leaders can create a culture and the social norms of kindness within their organisational culture. As such, kindness in leadership pervades the culture of the organisation when the value of kindness is recognised. Moreover, Haskins argues that there is a significant justification for kindness which is that it can enhance the likelihood of boomerang kindness – a virtuous cycle. Kindness is not just a virtue but can also become a corporate value. Haskins and Thomas (2018) point out that there has been an increasing articulation of the importance of emotional intelligence, mindfulness and compassion and their positive role in organisations. They are seen to be important in alleviating stress and encouraging greater awareness of emotions, feelings and wellbeing. Added to this, attributes like collaborative teamwork and interpersonal reality are also seen to contribute to positive performance.

An example of kindness in the higher education sector is outlined by Lalit Johri (2018) who writes that as a faculty member of the Said Business School at the University of Oxford his life has been influenced by acts of kindness. Since having invasive surgery twice in five years, each time, his colleagues in the School ensured that he received the best aftercare during the recovery period. He followed this up in an exploratory study of 47 senior leaders based in emerging and developing countries, the objective of which, was to map the prevalence of kindness-based practices. From Johri's study the most frequently mentioned kindness-based behaviours were treating others with respect; caring and being responsive; communicating using a personal touch; adopting a humane approach; listening intently and explaining logically; sharing information in a transparent way; accommodating personal issues or circumstances of others; valuing the views of others; and counselling and being an inclusive leader. Whilst Haskins (2018) is of the opinion that key attributes of leaders who are kind include compassion and care, empathy, altruism, respect and fairness. Additionally, Haskins and Thomas (2018) note that a number of virtues (compassion, gratitude, humility and humour) are also characteristics of the servant leadership approach which combines a motivation to lead with a motivation to serve. Haskins highlights that the wellbeing of individuals, organisations and communities will improve, if leaders demonstrate that they care and develop themselves and others to show respect to all who work within the organisation. Thus, treating everyone as equal in order to appreciate diversity and different views. Proposed practical suggestions include being authentic, showing gratitude, not trying to control everything and consistently practicing kindness. Kindness in a leader can transform this micro individual virtue into a macro corporate value (Mayer 2017). Moreover, kindness can positively transform individual relationships and helps create greater cooperation in teams. Kindness is seen as quiet leadership.

Summary

This chapter highlighted that conversation and dialogue are ways to unveil and test out ideas and thoughts with others. This involves reaching out externally to a network of friends, colleagues or professional mentors. However, it is only possible through building relationships built on trust. In this type of relationship, it is possible to be vulnerable, share deep and meaningful dialogue and modify assumptions being made. Additionally, practicing kindness was discussed as a virtue that enables leaders to transform both their relationships and the culture in which they operate within. It is the conversational leader who reaches out to talk to trusted others in an external capacity and by doing so finds resilience.

EXERCISE – FOOD FOR THOUGHT

1. Do you have trusted individuals you can turn to in times of crises?
2. Would you be prepared to reach out to a professional mentor or coach?
3. Are you building relationships built on trust?
4. Are you able to open up and be vulnerable in times of need?

References

April K A (1999) Leading Through Communication, Conversation and Dialogue, *Leadership & Organization Development Journal*, 20:5, 231–241

Brown B (2012) *Daring Greatly: How the Courage to Be Vulnerable Transforms the Way We Live, Love, Parent, and Lead*, Penguin, London and New York

Goleman D, Boyatzis R & McKee A (2004) *Primal leadership: Learning to Lead with Emotional Intelligence*, Harvard Business School Press, Boston, MA

Gurteen D *In Conversation: Learn to Listen and to Tell the Truth* (Gurteen Knowledge) www.gurteen.com/gurteen/gurteen.nsf/id/listen-truth Access February 2021

Haskins G, Thomas M & Johri L (2018) *Kindness in Leadership*, Routledge, Oxon and New York

Haskins Cited in Haskins G, Thomas M & Johri L (2018) *Kindness in Leadership*, Routledge, London and New York

Haskins & Thomas Cited in Haskins G, Thomas M & Johri L (2018) *Kindness in Leadership*, Routledge, London and New York

Johri Lalit (2018) Cited in Haskins G, Thomas M & Johri L (2018) *Kindness in Leadership*, Routledge, London and New York

Mayer (2017) Cited in Haskins G, Thomas M & Johri L (2018) *Kindness in Leadership*, Routledge, London and New York

Neenan M (2018) *Developing Resilience: A Cognitive-Behavioural Approach*, Routledge, Oxon and New York

Young J (2018–2019) *Research Interview Insights from Leadership and Resilience Study*, The Creative Digital Community, North East, UK. Research first published in this volume

8

TAPPING INTO CREATIVITY FOR WELLBEING

Creativity is subjective, out-of-the-box thinking and involves the ability to stretch and become experimental without worry of failure. New management literature is beginning to emerge to bring together creative aspects with arts-based learning for management. In terms of resilience and creativity, we need to learn that leaving time and space for creative exploration, self-awareness, and inner introspection and reflective practices pays dividends.

Less is more!

The key word is "allow" because sometimes being frenetic and busy is perceived as what you are supposed to do. In fact, allowing yourself more quiet time permits you to cut off from frenzy and this enables creative ideas and solutions to come to the forefront. It is a hard lesson to learn but less is more! In our world we have been brought up to think that showing that you are busy is important but flipping this notion allows a flow of creativity to emerge.

DOI: 10.4324/9780367280970-8

Letting go, being and finding yourself

Creativity can really flow and flourish when you let go of analytical thoughts and come into your own within the moment. This is called "being" – just be, be yourself. As mentioned in an earlier – chapter, tap into the inner knowing intelligence that resides within you. Be your unique self! Why be anyone else? De-layer to speak from a deep place. Just like an onion, de-layering, is opening up to the core and the DNA of your being. Why be a faux self or a part of imposter syndrome? Why place so many layers of protection around yourself? To be creative it helps to be in the moment, be yourself, allow experimentation and the flow of ideas. Creativity can be developed in an individual or when working in a team.

Follow the energy – what brings you energy?

Being balanced enables us to flourish and it is a leader's job to find a balance that suits their circumstances. Cameron (2016) suggests that creative energy is perhaps a form of spiritual electricity or the flow of good orderly direction. Knowing you have energy (being naturally in the flow) and more importantly, appreciating what brings you energy can be key in terms of finding your equilibrium and self-ease. Chopra (2020) believes that you can feel your way through life by receiving messages about your own behaviour as sensed by your body. He talks about this in terms of non-verbal messages delivered in chemical form which are signs of discomfort and trouble ahead or signs of wellbeing. Signs of trouble for Chopra include pain, physical discomfort, tightness and tension in muscles, headache, lower back pain and stiffness, nausea, insomnia, lethargy and fatigue. Whilst signs of wellbeing include lightness, energy, physical flexibility, good muscle tone, sound sleep, good digestion, absence of colds and flu, bright eyes and dynamism. Chopra believes that reading what your body is trying to tell you allows you to feel your way to healing earlier rather than later. The interviewee study highlighted the importance of being aware of your energy levels.

One interviewee describes sensing being run down.

> *"So, if we take the notion of energy, for me, there is one perspective where we sense that the batteries are run down, and that we are run down. We all have reserves, and we have*

> *reserves that we can call on where the battery manager just doesn't work – far deeper than what we believe we have. Actually, we all have limitations, and the bottom is there."*
>
> Male, experienced Creative Digital Executive Coach

This interviewee goes on to talk a lot about getting close to the edge whilst at the same time noticing the symptoms and energy. Again, this leader talks about recognising leadership resilience in terms of living with the uncertainty and the belief that you will get through.

Noticing the body's symptoms and energy

> "There have been a number of times in my life, probably just over a handful where I've had to take time out, not necessarily big time out [pause] touch wood here! But what I've noticed is that I have certain symptoms in my body when I am getting close to that. So, if I can detect the symptoms, I can come out of it before I get so far down into it."
>
> "It's not only emotion for me because there's a physical – it's physical, it's a physiology."
>
> Male, experienced Creative Digital Executive Coach

The message is undoubtedly, follow the energy to be in the flow. Being aware of your energy levels helps you to detect and pre-empt a fall. Ask yourself, what brings you energy? The spirit is linked to the energy that we create for ourselves. Being in the flow helps with the creative juices.

Creating a sacred space for creativity

Creating a sacred physical space supports your ability to tap into inner creativity. A quiet space is a place to go to – this is all about creating your own zen retreat. A space where you can go to rest and relax, special to you. What does sacred space and creativity mean for you? Can you find the time? Do you allow yourself to be experimental? Do you allow yourself to reflect? Some individuals cannot allow themselves time, whilst others don't want to be with themselves for too long. In the hustle and bustle of life, leaders today need to allow themselves time for being in a quiet space in order to nourish and replenish self. Creative writer Julia Cameron suggests, "If you think of the universe as a vast electrical sea in which you are immersed and from which you are formed, opening to your creativity changes you from something bobbing in that sea to a more fully functioning, more conscious, more cooperate part of that eco-system" (Cameron 2016).

Creative space to activate wellness

It is hard to persuade the average individual that quiet time is precious and leads to more creativity. Chopra (2020) argues that quiet and inner peace are good experiences, but their real importance lies in escaping inner conflict, turmoil, fear, depression, worry, confusion and self-doubt. With practice, anyone can find this inner place, go there, and have the experience of a self that is whole and untroubled. Finding creative space for health and wellbeing is an important element for the resilient leader. However, spending time in a quiet space can allow the mind to let go, to jump across to a more creative place that permits you to be in the flow. As this occurs, you may find that new ideas arise in your mind, as quiet space refreshes the individual from the stress of daily activity. It can take various shapes and forms. Finding quiet space to retreat too, allows you space and time to connect to what Deepak Chopra calls a "sense of self." This is the timeless quality within, that enables you to connect to your own inner world. This time spent, can help you retreat, nourish yourself, gain insights and creative know-how that will help you in times of need. It may be that quiet space requires a specially created space in your home for taking time out, or it could be a space outdoors that you walk too. Whatever form it takes, it is a place/space for introspection and letting go.

Re-connecting with self

> *"Nourishing may well be an appropriate word. So, the notion for me about resilience is partly about reconnecting and for me it is about spending time with myself, not spending time with other people."*
>
> Male, experienced Creative Digital Executive Coach

The examples from the interview research data highlight what tactics other leaders apply to enable wellbeing, and high on their agenda was "allowing time" for quiet space. Consequently, leaders discussed the difficulty of allowing themselves time in the fast-paced environment. Letting go allows you to switch off from everyday life and helps you to re-connect with your core being. Further techniques to support the switching off from daily activity include using meditation and mindfulness techniques. As such, it is little wonder that enlightened leaders today are being directed to meditation and mindfulness practices.

The inner teacher

How you think also has a major impact on your life. Inbuilt assumptions from past experience can negatively impact upon an individual's ability to move forward. Gallwey (2015) author of the famous *The Inner Game of Tennis* calls the conscious self "Self 1" and the unconscious automatic "Self 2." For Gallwey every game is composed of two parts, an outer game and an inner game. He starts with the assumption that the way "Self 1" talks to "Self 2" might hold the key to sporting success and failure and then asks: How do you stop self-judgement? How do you set the unconscious automatic mind free? How do you break bad habits, which are unconsciously executed and often carried out without any conscious reflection at all? Gallwey's views focus on implicit learning as a proposed solution: watching and thinking less; internalizing the visual image in front of you; experimenting with role playing and trying out different routines to increase the range of your game; playing and leaving Self 1 aghast at the goings on in this room of fun. Gallwey's broad approach is to be found in the Zen philosophy of "let it be."

Gallwey says it is the art of letting go of Self 1 control and letting Self 2 play the game spontaneously. In fact, he suggests it is locking Self 1 out of the room whilst gaining the experience of peace in the moment when the mind is relatively still, seeing the ball differently and listening to it and being aware of your breathing in the moment. The inner game takes place is in the mind of the player, and it is played against such obstacles as lapses in concentration, nervousness, self-doubt and self-condemnation. It is played to overcome all habits of mind which inhibit excellence in performance. Gallwey believes the player of the inner game comes to value the art of relaxed concentration above all other skills; finding a true basis for self-confidence and learns that the secret to winning any game lies in not trying too hard. He believes this process uses intuitive capabilities of the right and left hemispheres of the brain and as such unlearn bad habits in order to just let it happen. In short, getting it together requires slowing the mind. Quieting the mind means less thinking, calculating, judging, worrying, fearing, hoping, trying, regretting, controlling, jittering or distracting. It is the purpose of the inner game to increase the frequency and the duration of these moments, quieting the mind by degrees and thereby realizing a continual expansion of our capacity to learn and perform. Ultimately the winner in the end stops caring about outcomes and plays all out.

From the research a quote about the inner teacher and creating sacred space for dialogue and conversation in difficult times.

> *"So, we have an inner teacher, yes, but actually how do we create sacred space for that and how do we grow that in a way that's aligned."*
>
> Male Creative Digital Founder

Gallwey suggests that what makes the whole process of getting unstuck effortlessly is that you are dismantling a phantom in order to see who you really are. *The Inner Game of Tennis* highlights the technique of listening and observing in the moment. This is similar to Young's (2012) creation of the LOFT metaphor (listen, observe, feel and think) a personal knowledge awareness model within knowledge creation. The metaphor forms part of a personal individual knowledge perspective and helps guide the individual to find the know-how and wisdom that resides within them so that they can access, sense and gain a new quality of understanding through the boundless possibilities of the infinite intelligence (Young 2012). The LOFT metaphor encompasses listening, observing, sensing, feeling and thoughts, to achieve stillness, intuitive wisdom and self-mastery. The outcome in this respect is that the leader experiences knowingness and wisdom from an interior place of deep inner wisdom. Of course, the ultimate tool for accessing personal inner intelligence and know-how is through meditation.

Meditation

Meditation is a technique used to help switch off the chattering mind and may involve a mantra (basic sounds in Sanskrit). Meditation is derived from the spiritual techniques of the East and there are many different types. Chopra (2020) proposes that generically, meditation mode is any mental state that looks inward. Over the centuries, these mental states have acquired names including mindfulness; self-inquiry; reflection; contemplation;

concentration; prayer; quiet mind; controlled breathing and bliss. These practices belong to the art of meditation. Quiet and inner peace are good experiences, but their real importance lies in escaping inner conflict, turmoil, fear, depression, worry, confusion and self-doubt (Chopra 2020). Meditation is about mind, body and spirit as a continuous whole, not three separate things. In essence, Chopra introduces a view of meditation which is wider and more natural to grasp than focusing only on one element. One form of meditation uses a mantra or "a string of words" that are repeated again and again. The chanting of the mantra helps the mind turn off from everyday thoughts and allows stillness to enter the mind. This is an effective and powerful practice and over time helps the individual reach a calmness of temperament. Mantra mediation has amassed the widest and most far-reaching research of any mediation practice. According to Chopra benefits include the reduction in anxiety, lowered blood pressure, effective stress management and mind body benefits.

Corporate businesses also offer meditation to their workers. Gero (2014) stresses that everyone knows that meditation reduces stress. He argues that with the aid of advanced brain scanning technology, researchers are beginning to show that meditation directly affects the function and structure of the brain, changing it in ways that appear to increase attention span, sharpen focus and improve memory. Gero emphasises that a growing number of corporations, including Deutsche Bank, Google, Hughes Aircraft, General Mills and Aetna Insurance offer meditation classes to their workers. He highlights that meditation makes employees sharper and improves productivity in large part by preventing stress-related illness and reducing absenteeism. He also points out that business schools are also teaching meditation techniques to aspiring MBA's as well. This includes some of the executive MBA programmes in the US, teaching students to meditate and focus, from Harvard to Michigan's Ross School of Business to the Drucker School of Management.

Additionally, the research quotes from this study show that leader's focus on meditation and zen-type retreats. Meditation itself can happen in short bursts as emphasised in these quotes.

Valuing meditation

"I don't meditate, but I know a few of the guys in here (enterprise hub) who do. I think I'd quite like to learn. It is on my list to do, to try. I want to learn how to do it effectively.

> *You read books and you look at all the successful people and they all meditate. One of the guys in here actually had a nervous breakdown out of the blue, a happy go lucky guy, you wouldn't have seen it coming. Something triggered and he now meditates and learnt how to do it properly and he is a different person. He has these coping methods and he's fine now, he actively meditates, and he said it really helps."*
>
> Female, Creative and Entrepreneurial Business Manager

> *"I think we can meditate for very short periods and in all sorts of different locations. So, that is how I also see the value of spending half an hour by yourself, doing something properly."*
>
> Male, experienced Creative Digital Executive Coach

Running, meditation and sensing

The following leader discusses discovering running as a way of letting the energy flow, so that running becomes partly a meditative process.

> "Something that surprised me a few years ago was that I was just chatting before I had a massage with the masseur, and I got talking about running. I run simply because it is about being healthy. And when I described my experiences to her she suggested I was meditating when I was running which was a new dimension to me. I had always associated meditating with stillness and opening up and letting the energy flow, in that sense. So, it was a misnomer for me around how can meditating be part of an activity such as running. But, actually, it was true because I can run to a point of getting into a state where I will describe as my body runs itself. And that's just a wonderful state to be when it becomes effortless."
>
> "A lot of people will run to solve problems; I don't, I go to clear my mind. I go to reconnect with nature; I go to smell the air; breathe the air; see what's around me. That's the notion of sensing and reconnecting."
>
> Male, experienced Creative Digital Executive Coach

Additionally, Olsen (2014) asserts that the concept of self-awareness or knowing oneself is central to both yoga and leadership education. In fact, through yoga the physical activity part of meditation enables you to gain increased clarity, energy, flexibility, toning and psychic awareness.

Physical yoga

"So, I do yoga and I think I know my limits. So I know when I'm stressed I'll block out my diary, I'll book time in, just because I know if it's four or five meetings a day, every day, I know by the end of that week it's going to be tough and it's going to be awful. I do think it's really important."

Female Creative and Entrepreneurial Business Manager

The data acknowledges that leaders are using and valuing meditation and yoga techniques as coping mechanisms within stressful environments.

Mindfulness

Mindfulness as part of meditation is a technique derived from Buddhist tradition that through deep breathing techniques focuses upon the inner body, rather than just the mind. Supporting the observation of the inner body and how the body is feeling. It involves internal observing and sensing. Mindfulness meditation is a receptive practice, has roots in Buddhism and typically refers to practices that bring gentle, unbiased attention and awareness to the moment (Shapiro et al. 2009). The current technique derives from individuals within a modern Western context, including John Kebat-Zinn (1944); Thich Nhat Hanh (2016). It can be easy to rush along without stopping to notice anything. Paying attention in the present moment is part of mindfulness. However, paying attention to your own thoughts and feelings and to the world around you can improve your mental wellbeing. An important part of mindfulness is reconnecting with our bodies and the sensations they experience. This may mean waking up to the sights, sounds, smells and tastes of the present moment. Added to this, another part of mindfulness is an awareness of our thoughts and feelings as they happen moment to moment. Mindfulness is about allowing ourselves to see and feel the present moment. When we do that, we can positively change the way we see ourselves and how we live. Using this technique, helps us to notice signs of stress and anxiety earlier, which helps us to deal with them better. Mindful interventions can contribute to reducing rumination and worry. Chronic overload is dangerous over the long term. This is particularly important for business leaders. Mindfulness was highlighted in the research.

Activating wellness through mindfulness

> *"So, I do mindfulness meditation. So, I did a course in mindfulness-based stress reduction about four years ago. So, I do mindfulness meditation pretty much every day. So, I do that. I do my best to change my own sort of self-talk. In the middle of October I'm going on a three day retreat to North Wales which is based on the work of Parker-Palmer. So, what the centre piece . . . is about how to hold another human being in a sacred space and that is the most resonant and meaningful way that I have found to do that. So, this will be my third retreat that I have been on to a Zen Monastery for a weekend."*
>
> Male Leader

Long (2019) in an empirical organisational development study focused on interviewing leaders on mindfulness practice and highlighted the benefits and impact. This was a study of the lived experience of organisational leaders who had sustained long-term mindfulness practice. The first benefit included a better focus and improved performance; improved thinking; listening and collaboration; objectivity; improved self-regulation, self-observation, and enhanced patience. The second finding was increased awareness and amplified awareness that contributed to greater authentic leadership. The third finding was the leaders' ability to be able "to be the change" and to attain calm and clarity amidst complexity and unknowns. The fourth outcome showed participants relationships improved through the development of empathy and emotional intelligence. Finally, the fifth and last outcome was conscious decision-making improved by doing the right thing at the right time. Alternatively, Frizzell et al. (2016) empirical study based on 20 interviews of leaders showed ten significant themes. These included integrated/balanced leadership; greater self-regulation; commitment to the practice; enhanced self-awareness; improved work relationships; greater inner calm and peace; greater self/other-empathy and compassion; deeper listening and being present; motivated by a personal/professional crisis; more tolerance for ambiguity and uncertainty. Both studies demonstrated greater balance and calm, more self-awareness, deeper listening, greater empathy, and better work relationships. Both studies also showed emotional intelligence.

The following quote is derived from the Frizzell et al. (2016) study and shows the voice of a leader in the study. As a participant from Frizzell et al.'s research work explains: "And you know, I feel like I work hard, I am responsible. There are times when I say, 'okay, that is enough for today, shut the computer off because now I need my other time. If I don't have that, tomorrow is not going to be a great day because I am going to be tired or whatever'. So, having that wisdom to do that, which I could not do before." Female small-business owner and former senior healthcare executive Frizzell et al. (2016).

Additionally, an overview from Frizzell et al. highlights the need for vertical learning in our lives.

> *"Humanity faces unprecedented challenges such as climate change, terrorism, and water scarcity (Guillén & Ontiveros 2012). Humanity's collective future is every capable adult's responsibility. However, those of us who serve in leadership positions have greater responsibility and opportunity to help solve our most pressing global challenges and midwife a positive future. Currently, however, a gap exists between the demands of the global environment and the capacities of leaders to respond to challenges with innovative and collaborative action for a thriving Earth community. Consequently, leaders who yearn to contribute to real solutions will have to access more of their potential. Traditional ways of learning will not suffice. People must open their hearts and minds to practices that foster vertical learning, not with blind faith, but with genuine willingness to experience for themselves whether these practices make a real difference in their lives."*
>
> Frizzell et al. (2016)

The implications for positive change on the individual level are promising. The findings evidenced by these studies stress that mindfulness meditation has transformative potential for individual leaders who regularly, consistently and skillfully practice these techniques. Frizzell et al.'s final conclusions imply that leaders could use alternative techniques like mindfulness for vertical learning and survival in a tumultuous world.

Humour

Although humour was not a topic that arose in the research it may indeed be a factor in terms of resilience. Individuals with greater tendencies to use humour to cope (Lefcourt et al. 1990) and who report daily positive moods may have stronger immune system defences. In seems that the yogis of yesteryear knew this element as they created "laughter yoga" to get people to laugh more and thus change their mood and create a more positive tonic. Humour as a de-stressor is an undervalued resource.

Music as therapy for wellness

Music can not only be uplifting but can form a type of therapy for many people as part of wellness. Clinicians are now using music to soothe and calm patients, including those with dementia and psychiatric patients. Music has also been used to calm new-born babies (an example is the award-winning Lullaby Scheme by Music in Hospitals, Forbes 2017). Music has also increasingly been used in the military in both the USA and UK. Historically, by the end of World War II, community musicians were performing for thousands of veterans suffering war-related physical and emotional trauma. The wounded soldiers' consistent and positive responses to music led the military to examine the usefulness of therapeutic applications of music for wounded and disabled veterans (American Music Therapy Association 2014 cited in Gooding & Langston 2019). It is not surprising that data from the interview study suggested that some leaders used music for therapeutic means. Moreover, little wonder that the creative digital leaders interviewed were also listening to music for wellness practices through CDs and apps. Music is a healer and the deep and rich impact of beautiful music on the emotions is part of the agenda in the creative arts in management.

Summary

This discussion supports the development of the authentic individual who explores and listen to their inner ideas in order to find creativity, wellness and resilience. They may do this by finding a physical place or space for quiet mental introspection and listening that leads to creativity. In this way, a search for energy and creativity leads to self-awareness and to building on what brings joy and flow into our lives, rather than that which drains our energy. The leader who can associate with wellbeing through creativity and active engagement with personal inner awareness is a leader that could be described as creative. By using an array of meditation techniques to find balance, and to find answers from the inner self, a leader may benefit from the healing properties of a time/nexus quiet space. By using yoga, meditation and mindfulness techniques such a leader understands the impact of quiet time and space to tap into deep knowing for creativity. This leader is a Creative Explorer who is open to experimentation, finds time for creative outlets through quiet space for introspection, and alternative means that foster vertical learning, to access their potential.

MEDITATION PRACTICE

"Any experience that brings you into contact with the silent level of awareness can be called meditation. You may have spontaneously hit upon a routine that allows you to experience a deep settling in your mind. If you haven't yet, then you might adapt one of the more formal meditation practices that appear in every spiritual tradition."

Practice

"Sit quietly with your eyes closed in a room with the lights low and no distractions from the telephone or knocks at the door. Shut your eyes for a few minutes; then become aware of your breathing. Let your attention follow your breath as it gently, naturally draws inward. Do the same as the breath flows outward. Do not make any attempt to breathe with a certain rhythm and don't try to make your breath deep or shallow. By following your breath, you are aligning yourself with the mind-body connection, the subtle coordination of thought and *Prana*, the subtle energy contained in the breath. Some people find it easier to stay with their breathing if they repeat a sound: one syllable for the out breath, one for the inner. *Ah – Hum* is a traditional sound useful for this purpose (you can also adopt mantras).

Perform this meditation for 10–20 minutes twice a day. You will become aware of your body relaxing."

Reference: Chopra (2004) The Book of Secrets: Who Am I? Where did I come from? Why am I Here? Rider and Random House Publishers

References

American Music Therapy Association (2014) *Music Therapy and Military Populations: A Status Report and Recommendations on Music Therapy Treatment, Programs, Research, and Practice Policy*, musictherapy.org/research/music therapy_and_military_populations. Cited in Gooding L F & Langston D G M M (2019) Music Therapy with Military Populations: A Scoping Review *Journal of Music Therapy*, 56:4, 315–347

Cameron J (2016) *The Artist's Way: A Spiritual Path to Higher Creativity*, Souvenir Press, London

Chopra D (2004) *The Book of Secrets: Who Am I? Where Did I Come from? Why am I Here?* Rider and Random House Publishers, London

Chopra D (2020) *Total Meditation: Practices in Living the Awakened Life*, Random House Publishers, New York, Harmony Books

Frizzell D A, Hoon S & Banner D K (2016) Phenomenological Investigation of Leader Development and Mindfulness Meditation, *Journal of Social Change*, 8:1, 14–25

Gallwey W T (2015) *The Inner Game of Tennis: The Ultimate Guide to the Mental Side of Peak Performance*, Pan McMillan Publishers, London

Gero J (2014) *Meditation & Leadership Do Meditators Make Better Leaders?* Leadership Excellence Essentials Presented by HR.com

Gooding L F & Langston D G (2019) Music Therapy with Military Populations: A Scoping Review, *Journal of Music Therapy*, 56:4, 315–347

Guillén & Ontiveros (2012) Cited in Frizzell D A, Hoon S & Banner D K A (2016) Phenomenological Investigation of Leader Development and Mindfulness Meditation, *Journal of Social Change*, 8:1, 14–25

Kebat-Zinn J (1944) *Defining Mindfulness* www.mkindful.org/jon-kebatt-zinn-defining-mindfulness Access 11 January. Cited in Haskin G, Thomas M Johri L (2017) *Kindness in Leadership*, Routledge

Lefcourt H M, Davidson-Katz K & Kueneman K (1990) Humor and Immune-System Functioning, *International Journal of Humor Research*, 3, 305–321

Long B (2019) The Lived Experiences of Long-Term Mindfulness Practitioners – Dissertation Cabriai University

Music in Hospital and Care, Lullaby Hour Scheme, North East Region (Forbes A 2017)

Thich Nhat Hạnh (2016) *How to Love*, London, Rider, Penguin Co. UK

Olsen P E (2014) Namaste: How Yoga Can Inform Leadership Education, *Journal of Leadership Education*, 13:1, 116–125, Winter

Shapiro Carlson & Kabat-Zinn (2009) Cited in Frizzell D A, Hoon S & Banner D K A (2016) Phenomenological Investigation of Leader Development and Mindfulness Meditation, *Journal of Social Change*, 8:1, 14–25

Young J (2012) *Personal Knowledge Capital: The Inner and Outer Path of Knowledge Creation in a Web World*, Chandos/Elsevier, Oxford

Young J (2018–2019) *Research Interview Insights from Leadership and Resilience Study*, The Creative Digital Community, North East, UK. Research first published in this volume

9

DARK SIDE TO LIGHT

How dark can it get?

Leadership can take you to the edge! It can take you to a dark place. In times of crises, how dark can it get? We need to understand the many shapes that dark side leadership takes in order to assess our strategies and flourish. The questions many leaders may ask themselves are: How far will I crash when it gets really tough? Maybe this is followed by the question: Do I have the strength and resilience to carry on? For some individual's, life is consistent even though there are many highs and lows because they are comfortable with challenges. However, for many others, steady is not easily accomplished, and the journey involves "riding the waves" – the crashing waves that can crush and destroy, and the unexpected waves that roll over you. Whichever wave you experience you need to be steady in both the wind and breeze. How an individual responds to tough times will vary as we are all unique. How we respond in times of emergency is part of a reserve of strength gained through past experience, know-how, psychological resilience and mindset.

DOI: 10.4324/9780367280970-9

Dark side and leadership failure – the bad apple

There is no doubt that massive leadership failure pervades both business and society. Pfeffer (2015) thinks the leadership industry has failed. He discusses the difference between "feel-good" leadership and too many toxic workplaces pointing out that from an American/European perspective too much of the leadership industry has become a form of lay preaching by telling inspiring stories about heroic leaders and exceptional organisations. Pfeffer encourages everyone to stop accepting sugar-laced but toxic potions as cures. On a positive note, he suggests two ways to understand the many leadership failures. The first way is to understand the "bad apple" theory, where an individual is literally a bad apple. The second way is to explore the systemic processes that produce leaders who often behave differently from what most people might like or expect. In Pfeffer's view, leadership failure needs to be explored, if one cares about the enormous psychological, and even physical toll, exacted on employees from bullying, abusive bosses and work environments filled with multiple sources of stress. He suggests that there still remain many leaders stuck in the past, using styles of leadership that exploit power and therefore we need to remain cautious about the emergence of these types of leaders. This is a sharp reminder of the real world and the non-changing nature of man.

Feeling the terror and getting through it

Reaching a low point can cause extreme anxiety and in some cases terror for the individual. The following experiences were captured from the interview study. After being asked about climbing out of rock-bottom, interviewees said:

> *"You don't know what resilience is until you've hit the wall. And everybody can go 'yeah, yeah I'm resilient.' Really? Are you? How do you deal with that? It's a bit like asking somebody to go and deal with a close death, until it happens, you've no idea, and then it knocks you sideways. You can prepare yourself, but you know that it's nothing like the reality, and I think that we have to get out of this and we have to go much, much deeper, to get sustainability."*
>
> Managing Director of a creative company

> *"So, it's terror and it's basically feeling incredibly inadequate and it's feeling like, actually, you're making this situation worse and your ability to create value and make people happy*

and do things are aligned, that make you happy as well. It feels like it's getting further out of reach and you're going to run out of money and you're going to be defenceless and it's going to be shaming and you're going to fall apart."

Male Leader

"Just realising that I have got the support of a lot of people, realising that it's not the end of the world. The thing that I tend to do, and which is also a negative, is I tend to see everything at once, so I see all these different situations that may impact on what happens in 18 months' time, all happening now, rather than being a series of events. So I suppose one of the ways I try and force myself to emerge is to try and process them and unpack them. Go back to the basic principles of take some small steps towards it."

Male Chief Executive of a creative business

One entrepreneurial leader described feelings of inadequacy, whilst another discusses living with uncertainty.

"Failure. Epic failure. Darkness. Well, not darkness necessarily but feelings of inadequacy, failure and really falling short."

Male Leader

"Out of sync for me was close to rock-bottom in the sense of I thought I knew what I was about, but it was not what I was about, and I didn't know what it was that I was about. I didn't know what was part of me. That can be rock-bottom and it's an awful place to be. . . . I am thinking of people who have broken down in front of me: it isn't common but it's not rare. And when people literally break down and apologise for breaking down, literally there's floods of tears, it is because they are on the edge. They are on the edge of what's going on in their life. . . . There's also for me resilience cognitively. When something is such a concern that it worries us. It can chronically worry you. So, there is a resilience around coping with that worry because sometimes we can't resolve the worry, it's not within our gift to be able to sort things out, it's too complex, or whatever. So, it's about living with the unknown and living with the uncertainty. Resilience is therefore, believing that, 'okay, I will get through this."

Male, experienced Creative Digital Executive Coach

Darkside means different experiences for individuals. It can be a frightening experience and as noted it may make the individual feel negative. It means living with uncertainty. Hence, having support around you can make a real difference according to these leaders.

Internalised darkness, shadow, inadequacy and falling short

At the extreme end of the scale, let us not forget that leaders and founders relate failure so personally that they kill themselves. By internalising the external failure linked to themselves in the business environment they become broken by the emotional struggle. As the following statements illustrate, what they really need to do is kill the identity (persona) they have created, which is a different matter. Because, detaching from their business persona, may help them to just want to kill the identity itself, rather than the person.

> *"Okay, so people kill themselves and you know people are really passionate about stuff and they fail; and what happens is, they are beyond redemption and, therefore, they want to associate with that failure of the business because they're so invested in the business. They actually consider that because the business has failed, they are failures and, actually that they far beyond redemption and, therefore, they want to kill themselves or they want to kill this identity that they have created."*
>
> *"I don't think they want to take their own lives, but they just feel like they're bankrupt as a person, they're broken and that's the dark side, the shadow side. It's not really the dark side – it's like the shadow side of entrepreneurship – but it's the emotional struggle of entrepreneurship."*
>
> Male Leader

In particular, many entrepreneurial leaders take high levels of risk without being fully prepared. To survive they need to develop a mindset of change and flexibility where failure is expected. A strong buoyant personality can rebuff business failure and accept and embrace "fast failure." This type of mindset is a principle in the methodology of lean start-up (Ries 2011). The key aspect here is not to mentally internalise professional failures or setbacks but rather let them wash off quickly so that you move forward. For this reason, part of mental toughness involves embracing and expecting failure!

Within the research the following leader said it took up to six months to recover from a major blow, however, there was the constant going under, on a daily basis, that many individuals experience.

"It's a continual basis because you're sort of going down and then you're trying to recover and re-emerge, but then you're having to do it and you're saying that you have to do it on such a regular basis that that's very tough. It's not that it just happens now, and you go rock bottom, but that it is actually continual."

Male Leader

"I think that most of the time what we do is we just block out that feedback and we say it's someone else's fault and we don't take it upon ourselves because we don't actually have the machinery and the strength and the internal resources in terms of resilience and strategy; strategy to come back from that."

Male Leader

Toughness can be learnt but also comes from previous life experience which is unique to individuals as they climb through the low times to find an equilibrium. Detaching from the business persona and embracing fast failure are survival techniques.

The public crisis

Leaders interviewed – both male and female – described experiences whereby they were involved in a very public crisis. They talked about the extraordinary stress that this presented for them and one talked about still getting over this. One example is presented in this quote:

"We had a Board meeting, and it was announced we were going to be shut-down, effectively, immediately more or less. That for me was the first, obvious, very public professional crisis and it really did feel like a life-threatening ordeal professionally speaking of course. So, you know that was extraordinarily stressful and a difficult time and of course the near threat of that happening is enough to kill somebody in a sense and I'm sure that part of the strategy was just to shake the cage so loudly that we would all just more or less run away and think, 'Oh God we can't deal with this. That was a rock-bottom professional moment in my life."

Male Managing Director of a digital company

This leader described how he went on to reach out to a very high-profile Chief Executive to receive support.

Becoming stronger – learning and finding strength in the darkness

The following quotes were about becoming stronger after being wounded and ultimately learning from this experience.

> "So, for me it was the first time it happened – it was suffocating and demotivating and upsetting, although that is quite an emotive word, I do not do emotive words very often, but it was upsetting. The second time it happened I think it made me stronger. Certain things in my career have happened – that at first you feel slightly wounded but very quickly pick yourself up and become stronger for it and learn what not to do."
>
> "I found that going through a dark experience at work led to finding more strength and as such learning from the experience second time around."
>
> Female Entrepreneur

As mentioned, leaders were keen to learn from their experiences, find inner strength and suggested that what is required is being adaptable enough to live with uncertainty. In entrepreneurship, experience is highly valued as it builds up strength of character.

Darkside and types of pathologies and toxic disorders

For many, dark side means power, fear, depression and tears. It can mean reaching a time where hope diminishes. Pfeffer (2015) argues that if one cares about the enormous psychological and even physical toll exacted on employees from bullying, abusive bosses and work environments filled with multiple sources of stress – then failure in leadership needs to be explained. A lot has been written about the dark side from an entrepreneurship perspective. Notably, entrepreneurial leaders themselves need to evaluate risk very carefully. Kuratko (2007) discusses the dark side within entrepreneurship describing types of risk, the first is confrontation with risk (financial, career, family, social and psychic risk) where the question to be asked is whether the psychological impact may be too severe? The second type of risk expressed is entrepreneurial stress. A third element added included the ego, those have an overbearing need for control, a sense of distrust and an overriding desire for unrealistic optimism (Kets de Vries & Korotove 2007). Kets de Vries (2014) from a management and psychoanalysis approach outline and discuss the various types of pathologies and toxic disorders of executives. These include the: narcissist; manic-depressive; passive-aggressive and the emotionally disconnected. Each one of these types of disorders can be identified to some degree.

THE NARCISSIST: Narcissists have fragile self-esteem (despite their apparent confidence) and react poorly to confrontation. According to Kets de Vries, the real disease of many executives is narcissism, and he makes a distinction between reactive and constructive narcissism and believes there is a lot of varieties of reactive narcissism. He highlights that destructive narcissists often want to get even, and they can be exploitative, vindictive, totally self-centred and treat others as things rather than human beings. They lack empathy and lose their sense of boundary management as, according to Kets de Vries, they believe that the normal rules don't apply to them anymore. Moreover, the narcissistic personality disorder can show arrogant and haughty behaviours or attitudes: grandiose sense of self-importance and entitlement (Simonet et al. 2017). Narcissistic and antisocial individuals share a number of socially malevolent tendencies, such as callousness and exploiting and devaluing others. Hogan and Hogan (2009) suggest antisocial leaders lack the ambition of narcissists and labelled such tendencies as "mischievous," identified by risk taking, recklessness and limit-testing.

THE MANIC-DEPRESSIVE: Manic depression, or bipolar disorder, is another psychological condition that some executives suffer from. Like most disorders, it varies in intensity, but even relatively mild forms can derail careers and alienate friends and colleagues.

THE PASSIVE-AGGRESSIVE: This term describes a person who expresses negative feelings indirectly and shies away from confrontation. The behaviour originates in families where the honest, direct expression of desires is forbidden; children quickly learn to repress their feelings and are very reluctant to be assertive (Kets de Vries 2014). They go through life being outwardly accommodating but obstructive in an underhanded way. What is more, their feelings may be so repressed that they do not consciously realize that they are being un-cooperative. According to Kets de Vries (2014) passive-aggressive executives overtly agree to requests, but they covertly express their resentment of them by missing deadlines, showing up late for meetings, making excuses or even undermining goals. They tend to use procrastination, inefficiency and forgetfulness to avoid fulfilling obligations.

THE EMOTIONALLY DISCONNECTED: With this fourth type of pathology, a lack of feeling rather than an excess of it gives rise to difficulties. The term psychiatrists use for these people is alexithymia, which comes from the Greek and means "no words for emotions." Alexithymics would feel physically unwell rather than recognize emotional reactions. They do not understand why their body acts the way it does.

Appreciating the various types of disconnected, aggressive and emotionally lacking and toxic personality types we may encounter helps us to make our own assessment of the individual within context.

THE STORY OF THE PSYCHOPATH

The worst experience was when I was at the AK Consultancy company. I worked for a guy who, in hindsight, I think had psychopathic tendencies. So, that was absolutely the worst experience because my natural approach is to look for common ground, look for win/win solutions to try and work in a helpful and supportive way. And that doesn't work with somebody who's got that kind of psychopathic view of the world.

Some of the things around psychopaths are narcissism . . . very often psychopaths are lazy, so they don't do anything themselves, but they take a lot of credit for the work of other people. They are liars. So, they will say anything. It is not just the odd lie to get an advantage, or something; it is just a part of their makeup, basically, so they lie all the time. And the unpredictability, so there is the lack of empathy, not appreciating people's feelings and they do not care what they do. And because they don't feel empathy, they are able to play at it, they act it out and they use that as a way of manipulating people. So, that was definitely the worst experience that I've had from a leadership perspective.

How did you feel in that situation?

It kind of, over time, it just kind of eroded my confidence. I suppose that was the biggest thing. The unpredictability is really difficult to deal with. So, on a day-to-day basis you are always having to sort of second-guess things. The mood that he was in on the day would have a really

> *big impact on the kinds of things he would do, and things would just appear out of the blue.*
>
> *It was just extremely wearing but I think, also, it kind of raised my sort of anxiety levels and it certainly wasn't the kind of relationship where I was able to do my best. I think, ultimately, with that kind of person, they are always looking to undermine people and, eventually, to get rid of them. In effect, you know, they just have a very high turnover of staff. They don't trust people and you can't trust them. It's just a very toxic environment.*
>
> *What I really regret about that is that I didn't take action at the time. I mean, one of the things I could have done was record some of the conversations I had had with him. And that would have given me a really strong case to take that to the leadership of the organisation, or externally, you know.*
>
> *Male International Consultant and Coach*

Upon reflection this leader understood that saying no to unreasonable demands at work and taking action would have been appropriate because this type of behaviour can escalate as the psychopath (bully) continues when not called out.

Boundary violation and bullying at work

Abusive environments impact on the productivity and performance of staff. Workplace "abuse and incivility" decreases work effort, time on the job, productivity, and performance and consequently many employees are likely to quit their job. Employees may experience stress and depression with adverse effects on both their physical and mental health. Dark side experiences for some can include experiencing bullying at work that can take many forms. It can be in the form of passive aggressive language and be demeaning for those at the reciprocating level. It may also be a violation of boundaries. Kets de Vries (1989) acknowledges that narcissists lack empathy and can lose their sense of boundary management in the workplace as the offender believes that the normal rules do not apply to them. Jack's story was derived from the research study and highlights the abusive and toxic nature of bosses in the workplace.

JACK'S STORY

(Jack has an MBA and a is a Chief Executive working for a large UK corporate company.)

I worked for the B . . . Group and I was headhunted. I was actually quite flattered I suppose, the age I was at the time, getting headhunted. Yes, I was flattered. I was in my forties. To be honest it was probably time for a change. Anyway, I got headhunted, and yes flattered. Then the first 12 months or so were great because the guy in charge, the MD, he was very dynamic, he had some great ideas, and the current web experience was very rapid growth – maybe a bit too rapid looking back, but anyway it was rapid growth and our feet barely touched the ground. And the MD left to further his own personal interests and they, B . . . Group, brought in a new guy and everything fell apart from then on. Basically, whether this guy had had a bad experience with (B . . . Company) I don't know but he just took a disliking to all of us big style. Yes, I remember going down to the head office for a meeting, Maidenhead was the head office, so the national team were going for a meeting down there and I got there and he said, 'Can I have a word?', and I said, 'Yes sure,' and he said 'I'm not happy,' or whatever, so I said, 'What do you mean?', so he said, 'You're just poison,' I said 'what?' He said, 'You're a really sick Regional Manager.'

I said 'What do you mean? Explain.' He said, 'You're just poison, you're just sick, you're not good enough.' I said, 'Based on the grounds of what?' I said, 'What is it that you don't like?' He said, 'Just everything about you,' you know, and he was just sort of trying to have a go and every time I said, 'Well give me something specific then.' I said, 'You know it seems to me that you're having a go and you're giving me no opportunity, no sort of room for improvement in areas. Areas of you know what you expect from me, you've given me none of that,' so I said, 'come on then,' and then he said, 'I just don't like you basically,' and he said, 'You can go whatever.' I said well, 'what sort of timescale?' and he said, 'well now obviously.' So, I said, 'well do you know what it is – you have probably broken every rule in the book.'

I was respected within the company and then all of a sudden your credibility's challenged by a guy you have no respect for. All of sudden you feel like the chair has been kicked from underneath you. If it was something I'd done particularly wrong or I had been a bother or let

> *them down and underperformed – well I would have thought, 'well ok, you are justified in saying that.'*
>
> *However, systematically over a period of 12 months we all left, you know, we all sort of knew he was instrumental in making sure that the four or five of us were all ousted out. As I left the office, I walked up the road and I knew deep down that life would be better because I was better than that! Something deep inside of me told me that.*
>
> *It does knock your confidence no doubt, when some guy's calling you poisonous and sick and various other things, you think well, you've really got no grounds to say that. But it does make you question yourself to some degree and so my confidence took a bit of a hit, but there is no doubt at that point I just sort of rebuilt myself and I just thought well I felt really good.*
>
> *I thought it was a very extreme sort of way to react, with no justification, no evidence. I thought well if that is the way you think, nothing is going to change your mind. But it does knock your confidence and that was probably the point where I thought I really need to get out of this because this is grinding me down. I thought it was a personal slander. I felt a sense of relief when I left. I thought I am going to prove you wrong.*
>
> *So, the turning point for me was probably when I left there. I felt really down in the dumps, but it just gave me the drive and I tell you a lot was from thinking 'I'll prove you wrong,' you know, and I really did. I guess it gave me the motivation to re-assess myself and think well actually I need to move away from this life and go and do a job which is more fulfilling.*
>
> *Male Chief Executive of corporate company*

Jack moved on after about six months. He took time out to reflect before moving into a new position. He became a very successful business enterprise manager and director in future posts. However, this experience had left its mark, and Jack was close to tears as he relayed this story back acknowledging the pain it had caused.

Some aspects of bullying require "calling someone out." This may mean developing high-level communication skill sets that enable you to politely make a stand and say no to unreasonable demands at work. It may involve recording inappropriate comments and behaviour in a diary. An example of boundary crossing from the interview research is highlighted here:

> *"I've seen people, I've seen that person forwarding an internal email which is really sensitive to a really senior person in the organisation that the email was commenting about – and it was okay – so it was a boundary violation for me, so there's a boundary . . . more than a boundary crossing, it was a boundary violation. So, people will do things because they can get away with them and they're always testing the boundaries and they can do that."*
>
> Male Leader

Time and again people cross boundaries because they can and because no one calls them out or attempts to curtail their behaviour. All the more reason to make a stand.

Another story arising in the study was from a high-profile female who discussed a shockingly stressful situation that arose in 2017 when she got pregnant with her first child and decided to tell her new boss of one month. Within a month she found that she had been dismissed. Luckily, despite the stress involved, she kept her cool and received a lot of very strong support from family and colleagues who helped her to manage and navigate her way through resulting in multiple offers of employment. This was an abuse of power, discrimination and illegal. Unfortunately, this is still happening today.

Perceived nepotism, favouritism and cronyism in the workplace

New leaders bring their gang! Those favoured, friends and family. It happens so many times, again and again, as new leaders arrive in the workplace. It is breathtakingly normal. Studies by (Bellow 2005; Karakose 2014; Cingoz & Akilli 2015) highlight that some leaders disregard the natural basic principles of justice, fairness, and equality by favouring their relatives, friends and political cronies. This affects the business climate negatively and promotes corrupt behaviour (Akuffo & Kivipõld 2020). Favouritism is demonstrated with promotion of friends (cronyism) and family (nepotism) within the same organisation. It is perceived as not fair to the current staff who have bought into the system for promotion. A result of this will be resentment and bitterness. Soon those favoured by the leader are promoted! Another nail for those left out! It may just be that this promotion is honest, but if it is not perceived by staff as promotion by merit alone, then trouble is on the horizon. The consequence of this behaviour is that staff can individually or collectively thwart all efforts to move forward. Leaders need to be seen to be above favouritism. Leaders have to climb to a place where they are above reproach showing qualities of balance and honesty and being seen be open and transparent, because this way of working leads to trust and integrity being recognised. Perhaps the new leader is far more needy and vulnerable than they care to admit to themselves, otherwise why bring your own people? Mostly, this behaviour occurs because the individual leader is insecure! If they were secure in themselves with a strong sense of self, they would not have to bring in their own entourage. The impact on staff can be toxic. It begs the question – is this conscious or unconscious behaviour on the part of the new leader? Are they aware of the impact on staff? As a new leader coming into a business, it takes time for the troops to get to know how a leader operates, build the trust required, and learn to appreciate the transparency and fair play provided by the leader. Moving forward, organisations need to build authentic leadership and ethics into their leadership training programmes. Ethical behaviour and a strong internal moral compass can minimise the influence of nepotism, cronyism and favouritism.

Causes and cures of leadership isolation

Isolation involves leaders feeling separated from others and being left without peers – this may transform into isolation from reality. Leaders that suffer the anxiety associated with loneliness and disconnectedness may become careless of the feelings of others. They may be hugely grandiose, delusional and showing signs of loneliness of command. Kets de Vries (1989) theory suggests that those who feel isolated may find that isolation causes the following issues: loneliness of command; remoteness from reality; employees expecting magical powers of the leader; uncritical admiration by employees; grandiose behaviour; showing signs of aggression to depression.

Additionally, as isolated leaders find it harder to communicate, they become more insular in their behaviour. One leader discusses reaching a low point and feeling isolated in this quote which supports the isolation element Figure 9.1.

> *"It's quite depressing, it's quite low, and I feel a bit insular, that whole feeling of it is harder to talk about what's going on."*
>
> Male Chief Executive of a creative business

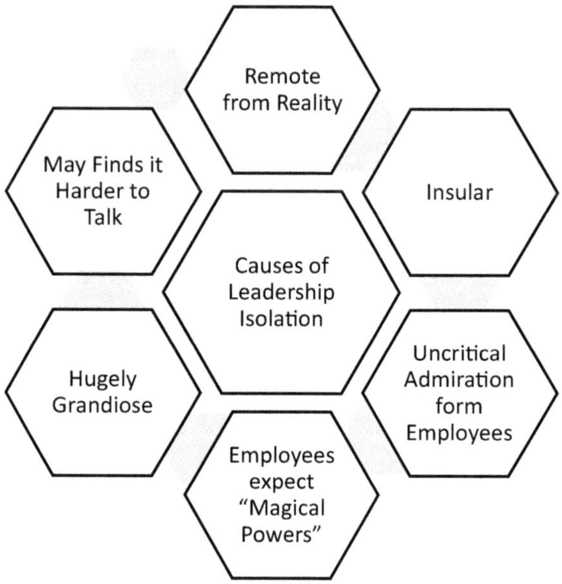

Figure 9.1 Isolation: adapted from Kets de Vries (1989)

Figure 9.1 has been adapted from Kets de Vries work and highlights causes of leadership isolation by including a lack of reaching out in the form of an inability talk.

Leaders can become isolated in their role. Kets de Vries (1989) talks in-depth about isolation and the causes, but equally highlights the safeguards. He suggests setting up safeguards to help cure part of a complex mosaic of interactive patterns. The first element – internal self-awareness – comprises critical self-evaluation; awareness of self; awareness of emotional reactions; and know-how to contain excessive emotion. The second element – internal organisation – includes feedback from colleagues; critical feedback from Board members and building relationships of equity, consistency and trust with frank exchanges. The third element – involves bringing in outside help – in the form of distribution of key policy decisions to members; bringing in consultants who have independent views and a less distorted vision and participating in top-executive training programmes. Additionally, isolated leaders find it much harder to communicate and any cure should therefore involve a means to reach out to trusted others for critical and reflective conversation.

Remembering – life is a gift

In addition to resilience and openness, the quality of adaptive capacity is an optimistic sense of can do and can try (Bennis 2013). Bennis goes on to say that "anyone who doesn't see the possibilities – well then, if you want to be blind, be blind." This interview quote reminds us that life is a gift.

> "Remembering is the one word that comes to mind. It is remembering. It is pulling the camera back and remembering that life is such a gift. It's the simple things again without sounding weird. It is the leaves and trees, and sky and the things that are just amazing. It is the reason I went into business because there is no upper limit."
>
> "When I am at the bottom, I think to myself . . . it's funny because what else can happen. It could always be worse"
>
> Male Leader

This interviewee described rounds and rounds of trying not to give up: "until the new baby arrives."

The simplicity of this example reminds us that being optimistic about the future is important and differentiating between business and personal chaos is important in terms of resilience.

Summary

Darkside of leadership is invariably linked to power. It is associated with leaders with no ethical compass losing their sense of integrity. It is not easy to find resilience in your darkest hour. Dark practices can arise in many shapes and forms in business and some of those aspects include the bad apple theory; pathologies and toxic disorders; nepotism, favouritism and cronyism; boundary violation and bullying. Appreciating the range of practices that come under the dark side label helps the leader to identify and assess the challenges ahead and consider how they may want to proceed. These issues have been elaborated, identified and evidenced by the quotes from study. Finding the individual resilience to address the dark times and move towards the light is discussed in the range of strategies offered for resilience in Chapter 10.

EXERCISE: READ THE STORY OF THE BROKEN PLATE

The story of the broken plate – aggression

Have you seen the broken plate? I came across it a couple of years ago and I thought it was really interesting. So, you say to somebody, 'here is a plate. I would like you to drop the plate.' The plate drops on the floor and smashes to pieces. Then you say, 'I'd like you to apologise to the plate.' So, you say, 'Oh, I'm really sorry, plate; I dropped you on the floor. Can you go back to how you were before?' Well, it is not possible. The plate cannot go back to its previous state.

And the analogy is that is what is happening in relationships inside organisations where somebody loses it with somebody, where they lose their temper, where they start shouting and swearing at them. Then they have broken a plate and quite often you hear people like that saying, 'well, I went back and apologised and as far as I'm concerned that's water under the bridge and we're back to where we were.' What about the other person? You know, you have just been in their face, you have been really aggressive. Do you think that they're just going to forget that the next time they have an interaction with you? Are they just going to think it's going to be exactly as it was before? That is going to damage communication.

That is the most vital thing in organisations. We need to be able to understand what is going on in other parts of the organisation, what customers think and what have you. So, you need to have that communication flow operating as smoothly and openly as possible. Every time people get into those aggressive situations, they damage the ability of that information to flow. Aside from the fact it is just not acceptable. I don't see how it is acceptable shouting and bawling at anybody.

Male International Coach and Consultant

EXERCISE – FOOD FOR THOUGHT

Read the story of the broken plate and self-assess.

- Do you have any broken plate stories?
- What might be the impact of bullying, pathologies or toxic disorders for yourself both personally and professionally?

- How best can you deal with this type of situation?
- Do you have contacts to reach out too in times of need?

References

Akuffo I N & Kivipõld K (2020) Influence of Leaders' Authentic Competences on Nepotism-Favouritism and Cronyism, *Management Research Review*, 43:4, 369–386

Bellow A (2005) In Praise of Nepotism: A Natural History, *Business Ethics Quarterly*, 15:1, 153–160

Bennis W (2013) Leadership in a Digital World: Embracing Transparency and Adaptive Capacity, *MIS Quarterly*, 37:2, June

Cingoz A & Akilli H S (2015) *A Study on Examining the Relationship Among Cronyism, Self-Reported Job Performance, and Organizational Trust*, The 2015 WEI International Academic Conference Proceedings, Vienna. Cited in Akuffo I N & Kivipõld K (2020) Influence of Leaders' Authentic Competences on Nepotism – Favouritism and Cronyism, *Management Research Review*, 43:4, 369–386

Hogan and Hogan (2009) Cited in Simonet D V, Robert P, Tett J F, Anastasia I A & Bartlett J M (2017) Dark-Side Personality Trait Interactions: Amplifying Negative Predictions of Leadership Performance, *Journal of Leadership & Organizational Studies*, 1–18

Karakose T (2014) The Effects of Nepotism, Cronyism and Political Favouritism on the Doctors Working in Public Hospitals, *Studies on Ethno-Medicine*, 8:3, 245–250. Cited in Akuffo I N and Kivipõld K (2020) The Influence of Leaders' Authentic Competences on Nepotism Favouritism and Cronyism, *Management Research Review*, 43:4, 369–386

Kets de Vries M F R (1989) Leaders Who Self-Destruct: The Causes and Cures, *Organizational Dynamics*, 17:4, 5–17

Kets de Vries M F R (2014) Coaching the Toxic Leader: Four Pathologies That Can Hobble an Executive and Bring Misery to the Workplace – and What to Do About Them, *Harvard Business Review*, 101, April

Kets de Vries M F R & Korotove K (2007) Creating Transformational Executive Education Programs, *Academy of Management Learning & Education*, 6:3, 375–387

Kuratko D F (2007) Entrepreneurial Leadership in the 21st Century, *Journal of Leadership and Organizational Studies*, 13:4

Pfeffer J (2015) *Leadership BS: Fixing Workplaces and Careers one Truth at a Time*, Harper Collins Publishers, New Yok

Ries E (2011) *The Lean Startup. How Constant Innovation Creates Radically Successful Business*, Penguin Random House, London

Simonet D V, Robert P, Tett J, Foster A I A & Bartlett J M (2017) Dark-Side Personality Trait Interactions: Amplifying Negative Predictions of Leadership Performance, *Journal of Leadership & Organizational Studies*, 1–18

Young J (2018–2019) *Research Interview Insights from Leadership and Resilience Study*, The Creative Digital Community, North East, UK. Research first published in this volume

10

PERSONAL RESILIENCE STRATEGIES FOR LEADERS

Internal and external wellbeing

Internal and external strategies for personal resilience: practising holistic wellbeing

Resilience is about finding the strength within to carry on. Personal resilience involves both an internal and external component. This involves tapping into the unique psychological strength that resides within the individual and taking pro-active preventative action. An inner and outer resilience supports a view of individual resilience which builds a holistic approach. As individuals we are made up of "mind, body and spirit" and each interacts and connects to makes us who we really are.

The following quote from the interviewee highlights

Work-life balance and escapism

"I think you've got to have an element of escapism. I don't have enough of a work life balance, but I do switch off when I'm at home. I rarely take work home at weekends. I am not one of these that work seven days a week, 24 hours a day. I think you've got

DOI: 10.4324/9780367280970-10

to switch off. I think that you have to do things that are right for different people, that enable you to switch off."

Male International Coach and Consultant

These leaders talk about escapism, and involvement in relaxation activities to help them clear their head. The ability to switch off is important and to have a rounded view of the meaning of life by practicing work life balance.

INTERNAL STRATEGIES

Life experiences

We all have a range of unique life experiences which shape who we are. Our ability to become resilient is partly formed from these experiences. Learning from life experiences is central to knowing who you are and your development and effectiveness as a leader. "If people are capable of learning from their experiences, they can acquire leadership" (Northouse 2007). In part, we may have to unlearn some of our responses. Similarly, leaders need to continually learn from their management experiences in order to make new decisions, bounce forward and not repeat the same mistakes.

Tapping into your intuition and knowingness

Tapping into your interior helps you to link to the essence of who you are. When the human spirit is not aligned to self, negativity floods in and depression maybe the result. As such, being aware of your emotional make-up and what it is telling you is very important. Leaders need to be in a positive space to cope with the highs and lows of life in an even and balanced way. Getting in touch with your spirit and inner resilience sometimes demands quiet and creative space. Less is more! Spending quiet time with self can encourage a strong link with your inner world, emotions and importantly your creativity. It is in this realm that we experience knowingness, gut feel and intuition. This may arise from that deep interior knowledge and knowingness that Polanyi (1967) talks about. This deep interior knowledge arises in individuals as a type of instinctive knowing of what feels right in a particular situation or context. Many times, this can save lives in times of terror and confusion and is a very useful internal tool for leaders and anyone who can grasp the significance of deep interior knowingness. The creative digital

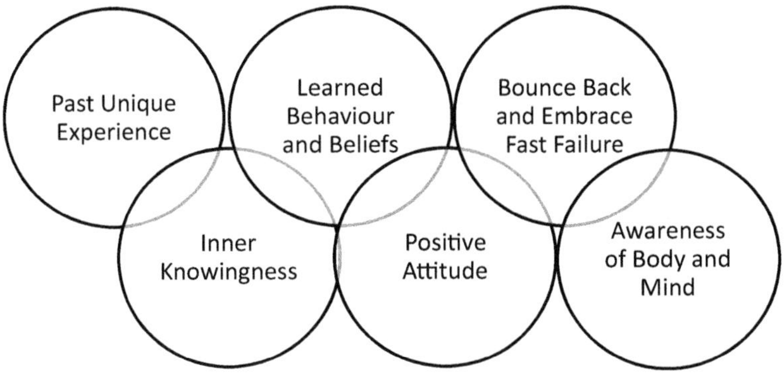

Figure 10.1 Applying our inner resources

Source: Young (2018–2019)

leader respondents discussed this element as an important part of their strategies as discussed in Chapter 4. Additionally, it was also suggested that you may need to find a quiet space to listen to the inner knowingness and intuition. The previous discussion is highlighted in Figure 10.1.

The psychological driver and mindset

The interviewees talked about mindset. In order to survive a certain amount of flex (flexibility and agility) are necessary. Those who have ingrained fixed views about the world will find it hardest to adjust to the constant change around them. Attitude and (meaning) is at the heart of resilience Neenan (2018). Whilst those leaders who appreciate the need for fast failure and dynamic change and realistically pre-prepare for this, will be the ones who are best prepared to survive in business. Discussed further in Chapter 6.

Positivity and mind-set

Taking positive steps is part of positive psychology as discussed by both Seligman (2011) and Fredrickson (2009). Positive psychologist Seligman (2011) emphasises the need to think in a positive light and wellbeing takes the centre stage as happiness (or **P**ositive Emotion) becomes one of the five pillars of Positive Psychology, along with **E**ngagement, **R**elationships, **M**ean ing and **A**ccomplishment – or **PERMA**, the permanent building blocks for a life of profound fulfilment. One-way people experience positive emotions in the face of adversity is by finding positive meaning in ordinary events and within adversity itself (Folkman & Moskowitz 2000; Fredrickson 2000b). Fredrickson proposes that positive emotions not only feel good in the present, but also increase the likelihood that one will feels good in the future. The broad and build theory (Fredrickson & Joiner 2002) encourages individuals to discover novel lines of thought or action. The solutions involve focusing on what is going right, focusing on strengths, learning to live with an ideal ration of 3:1 positive verse negative emotion and thus learning to find the gold in challenges. The suggestion is that joy creates the urge to play, and interest creates the urge to explore and encourages flexible and creative thinking that facilitates coping with adversity. The effects of positive emotions and positivity should accumulate, compound and amalgamate into what has been called a bank of positivity that turns into valuable psychological capital.

Awareness of body and mind

Inner personal resilience can also be supported by listening to our emotions and what they tell us about our current situation and acting on this. This involves an awareness of the essence of who you really are and deeply links to your emotions. The other point of reference is to be aware of is the physiology of the body, as it is the body that tells you in its own unique way, using a series of cues that you need to be aware of. By observing the cues both mentally and physically you can track the triggers that are crucial for you.

EXTERNAL STRATEGIES

Reaching out

We have already established that a first port of call for resilience is reaching out to a confidante and being proactive about this. There is an outer element of resilience in the form of inter-connection with those around us to look for support through conversation and dialogue. This can be through trusted individuals or professionals that you respect and can support you. Resilience may involve external experiences including the powerful tactic of reaching out to friends, family and professional contacts to have conversation and dialogue and explore and share the mental models, assumptions and ideas that we have built up in our minds. This requires frank and honest exchanges and critical and reflective conversations. This involves reaching out to those to whom you deeply trust and involves your ability to be vulnerable in the process so that conversations involve integrity. At times, it may involve checking in with a trusted other to check out your ideas and be challenged, in this way, becoming become less vulnerable.

Recruiting others into battle

It is essential to engage others right from the start to join your battle to put your career back on track. Friends and acquaintances play an instrumental role in providing support and advice in the process of recovery (Sonnenfield & Ward 2017). This is because those who care can help you gain perspective on the good and bad choices you have made. Sonnenfield and Ward highlight that you are more likely to make yourself vulnerable with those you trust, because without vulnerability you cannot hope to achieve the candid, self-critical perspective you will need to learn from your experience. In this respect, Sonnenfeld's study points out that slight acquaintances may be more helpful than close friends in steering you towards new opportunities. "People who can create connections are more likely to engender the kind of help they need when fate turns against them" (Sonnenfield & Ward 2017). The underpinning ethos in this approach is that discussion and dialogue are at the heart of resilience and that connection with others and building trustful relations is imperative to survival. Neenan (2018) points out that you might see help from others as a sign of weakness, however, he goes on to say that seeking the views of respected others can help you clarify where you are in the process and that resilience is not developed in total isolation. Whilst resilience is your own individual response – its development can be facilitated or impaired, respectively, by factors such as having supportive friends or experiencing violence from your partner (Neenan 2018). "If you know that someone could provide valuable advice in your time of need, seek it. Such support and advice can significantly reduce the duration of your struggle to overcome your problems. Therefore, a balanced view of self-reliance includes both self and social support" Neenan (2018). Therefore, resilience is best understood by taking in the wider aspects of life.

The data from the research highlighted the importance of reaching out to find a support network around you. This includes family and friends and critically trusted others. The following quotes express some of these views.

Reaching out and the support network

"So, I think it's about who you surround yourself with, it's about who is in your circles. I think it has a huge, huge impact on your outlook and the way you think, your mind-set you know all of that and I've got strong views about if you're the smartest person in the room then, you know, you're in the wrong room and that kind of thing."

"There are businesses in here (business entrepreneurial space), where they actually sit here and say, "basically, we're about to lose everything, if we don't get money into the business then it's game over." You know you're talking hundreds of thousands and it really impacts their mental health, and you have to have that dialogue with them and converse with them constantly, check in on them and I think that if they've got that support network in place it is a lot easier to get out of that rock bottom place (entrepreneurial space)."

Female Business Manager

"Times with family are important."

Male Creative Digital Entrepreneur

"I think having strong mentors/confidants around me has been really important. I think just having those sound boards, sometimes, has been a big deal for me. I think if I did not have that then, yes, I would maybe have gone off in certain directions."

Female Digital Consultant

The informal conversations could be with board members, business group/ network or a professional coach. The key to this is having both informal and formal conversations. In the interview research some leaders discussed meeting informally after work to share their thoughts with a confidante. Reaching out also requires opening-up to show your vulnerability as discussed in Chapter 6. This is portrayed in Figure 10.2.

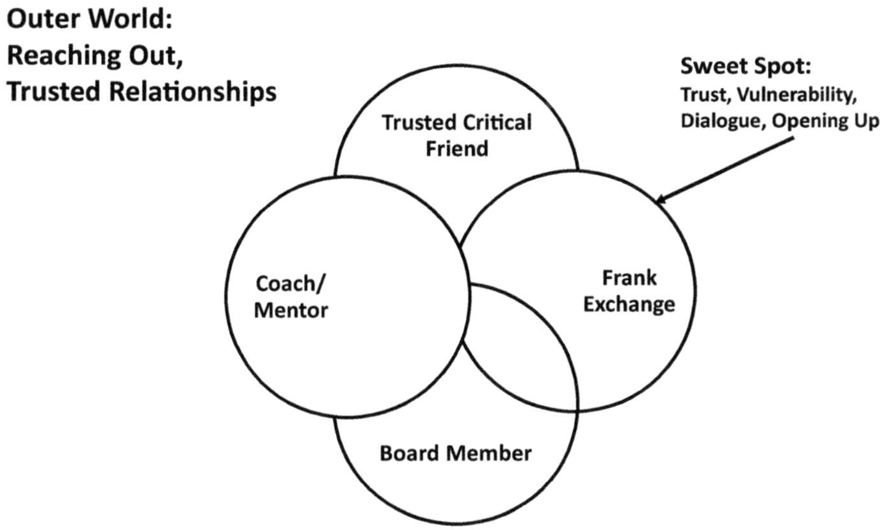

Figure 10.2 Reaching out to converse and be vulnerable

Source: Young (2018–2019)

Preventative physical activity

Resilience may involve pre-preparing your body and thinking preventatively to de-stress through exercises and activities such as running, walking, cycling, swimming, gym and cricket. All of which are ways to de-stress and keep the work-life balance. This involves being preventative in terms of identifying methods to exercise and find creative practices to de-stress regularly and tap into your creativity. Data from the respondents in this research highlighted that many are being pro-active and use a variety of ways to do this from exercising regularly, to using relaxation and calming activities including an awareness of good sleep and diet. All the respondents in the research interviews discussed their physical activities as part of the preventative exercises that became one of the main aspects of resilience.

Quotes from the leadership interviews discuss fitness as the antidote to stress, the saviour!

> *"But there is a broader thing as well you know – the mental state and your physical state are really closely interlinked. I think if you do not maintain your fitness then that has a*

negative impact on your sort of mental state. And there is something as well about just spending some time doing physical activities that gives you an antidote to stress."

Male International Coach and Consultant

"It has been my saviour in some ways because I said quite recently to someone – it's the only thing I do that's just for me. Coming back to your question, the true benefit from going to the gym is not physical it's more mental."

Male Creative Digital Entrepreneur

"So, I don't go (running) to solve problems; a lot of people will run to solve problems; I don't. I go to clear my mind. I go to reconnect with nature; I go to smell the air; breathe the air; see what's around me. That is the notion of sensing, reconnecting."

Male, experienced Creative Digital Executive Coach

"I very much feel that you have to be physically and mentally strong. You have to exercise; you have to keep your mind and body fit; and eat well. I just can't stress that enough because you push yourself through so many things, mentally, that if those other things aren't working the whole thing can just fall. Things like male suicide; things like heart attack can happen so if you're not mentally strong and physically strong to stop the heart attack because they are all linked."

Male Digital Founder

Figure 10.3 shows some of the preventative physical activities undertaken by leaders in order to prevent stress in the future derived from the interview research.

Wellness and therapeutic activities

Preventative therapeutic activities were also highlighted in the interview data. These activities included those leaders who said they took time off to go on a retreat whether one day at the spa or three or four days away from the office. The wellness strategies also included doing yoga exercises, spending time on mindfulness and meditation and listening to apps and CDs for relaxation. These leaders were aware that quiet time was necessary to step out of the hustle and bustle of everyday life. One leader talks about "allowing" oneself the time to do these activities, which is quite poignant and goes back to a mental process whereby time out is valued rather than being frenetic. It is important to have a private quiet space that you can retreat too,

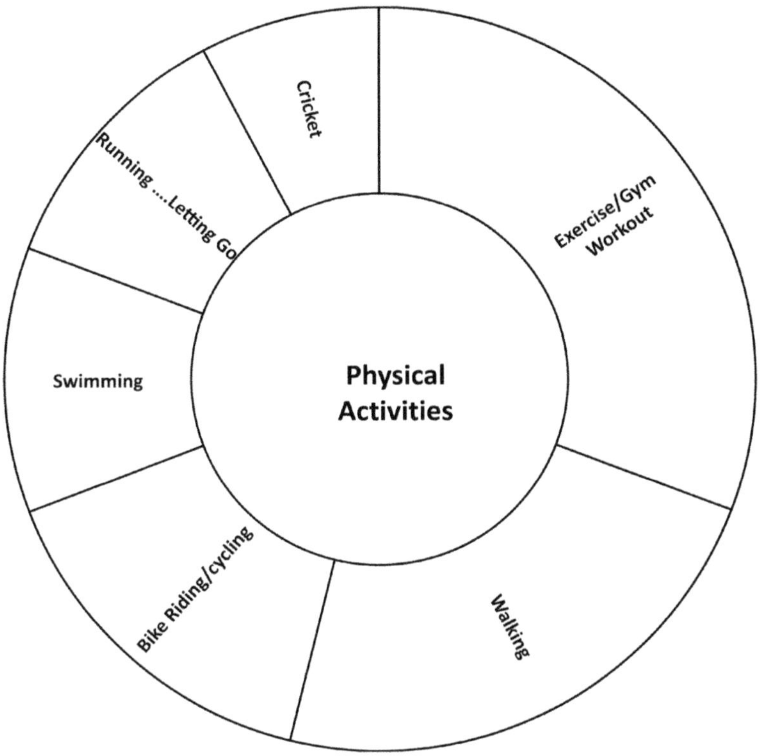

Figure 10.3 Preventative physical activities for personal resilience
Source: Young (2018–2019)

for instance it may be that you create a space within your own home to make your own. Or you may find a quiet space outside in the woods or by the river that is special to you. Consequently, having your own space helps you to cut off from the outside worlds as you connect to your own inner world.

Calm meditation apps

"Yes. I mean, I've got calm and head space meditation apps on my phone as well. So, going to bed with those. Taking ten minutes. Which is something that I put in place in the last few months that I've just been so mindful of, like, 'you're pushing too hard.' You said a great word for me which is 'allow'. I need to allow myself that time. And even if it is ten minutes just meditating in the morning before you start. Sometimes I start the run . . . start the day with a swim and stuff like that. Whereas, normally, I'd be really guilty starting with a swim, what if someone rings on the phone and what if you miss emails?"

Male Digital Founder

"I listen to podcasts every single day for at least an hour."

Male Managing Director of a digital company

Yoga

"So, I do yoga and I think I know my limits, so I know when I'm stressed so I'll block out my diary, I'll book time in, just because I know if it's four or five meetings a day, every day, I know by the end of that week it's going to be tough and it's going to be awful. I do think it's really important."

Female Business Manager

The data derived from the interviewees highlights the range of activity used to create inner calmness through therapeutic activity which form part of a mind, body, spirit approach. See Figure 10.4 derived from the data.

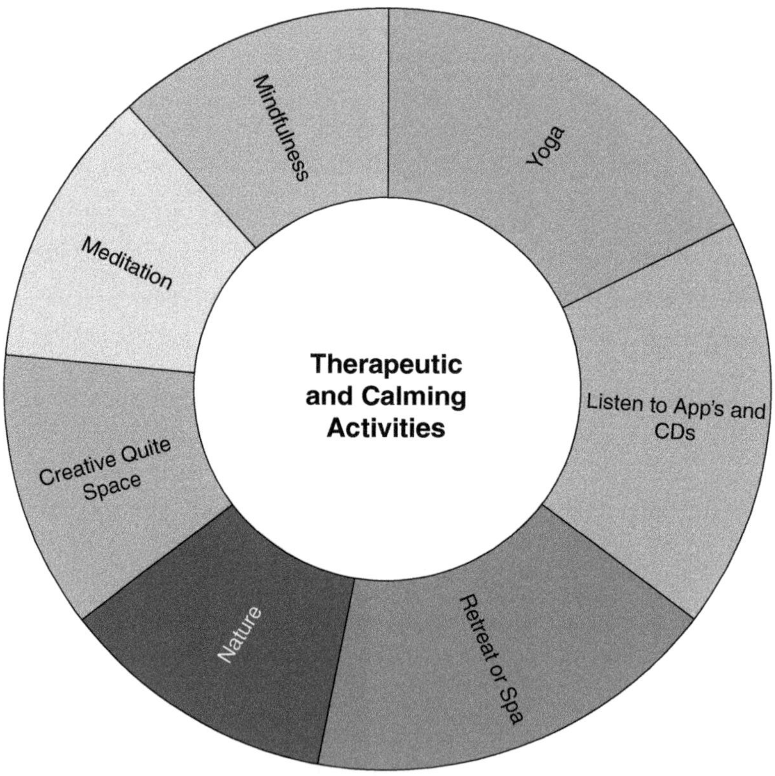

Figure 10.4 Preventative therapeutic and calming activities for personal resilience

Source: Young (2018–2019)

Relaxing activities

Additionally, the interviewees mentioned a range of relaxation and therapeutic activity that they undertake to enable them to be robust including doing the garden, playing with pets, cooking, family time, listening to music and inclusive of eating well and sleep.

> *"I am quite a fan of cooking, so I will spend Saturday mornings just cooking away . . . that is my thinking space."*
>
> Female Digital Consultant

> *"For some people it might be watching a movie, for some people it might be travelling, for some people it might be cooking, I don't know, you know, I think that I'm quite conscious about doing certain things that I know I can just clear my head."*
>
> Male International Coach and Consultant

Walking in nature

> *"For me, resilience is about being able to recognise that you are getting close to the bottom, or on the edge, or whatever; and then re-energising yourself. Right? It works different for different people, but for me the re-energising is reconnecting with nature, especially the sea. Those times when I've been experiencing being on the edge, I've often gone off to the coast and just either sat or walked by the sea as part of . . . sometimes it's only two or three hours, half a day, whatever, into the countryside. So, there's that side of it."*
>
> Male, experienced Creative Digital Executive Coach

An example of the types of activity are shown in Figure 10.5.

Other strategies, which have been discussed in previous chapters, include finding your own sacred space for therapeutic activities. As such, allowing yourself and others recovery time when appropriate as the body and mind need to recover from distress. Additional solutions include humour and appreciating that humour and laughter are therapeutic in themselves.

The body talks to you! Check-in and detect the symptoms in the body

Your body gives you cues and tells you how it feels. In this way it is forewarning you to take note. Are you aware of your body's cues and signs? It can be as simple as feeling emotional, tears swelling up, being irritable, cracks

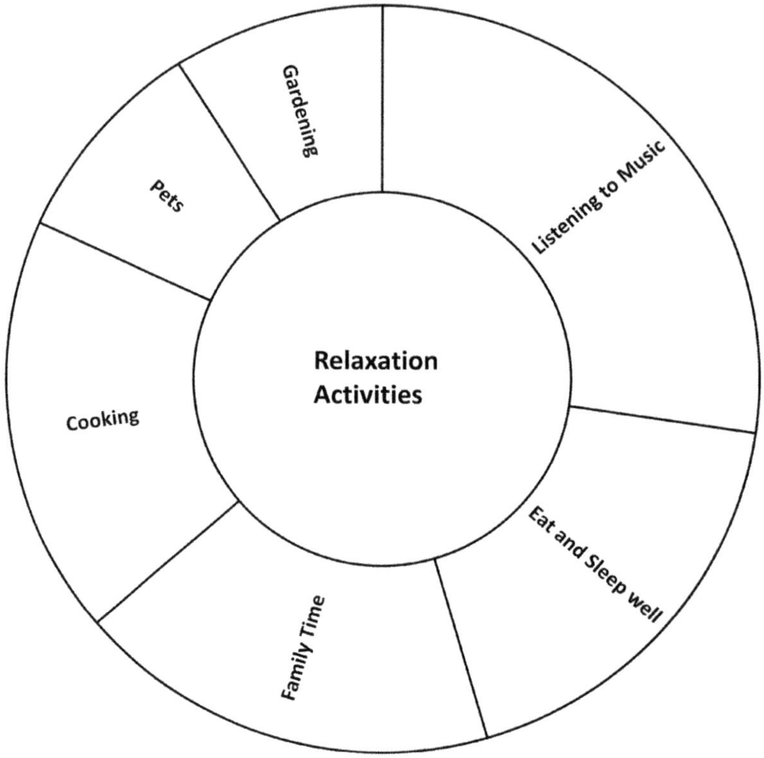

Figure 10.5 Preventative relaxation activities for personal resilience
Source: Young (2018–2019)

in the voice, tension headaches, stiff shoulders. The body is talking to you and letting you know that all is not well. Chopra and Tanzi (2018) point out that awareness skills can be used to improve your quality of life, and that the healing self becomes practical in any situation or any moment of the day. It monitors the signals that indicate your immediate state of wellbeing, here and now. This includes: knowing how you feel physically – involving being open and sensitive to the signals your body is sending; knowing how to interpret these signals – involving acceptance of the body as your greatest ally, not a source of distress, and knowing what is happening inside of you emotionally – involving giving up on denial, wishful thinking, fear and repressing your emotions. It is important to be aware of the signals that are unique to yourself. Awareness can help you make the necessary adjustments and capture this before it turns worse. This is especially important for leaders as part of self-awareness.

Noticing the body – meditating when running creates the energy flow

"So, If I can detect the symptoms, I can come out of it before I get so far down into it. . . . It's a physiology . . . Well for me, it is about how energy manifests itself in the body."

Male, experienced Creative Digital Executive Coach

"This eye is sitting twitching as we speak, so I know I need to sleep more, and you just have to listen . . . (to the body). It is about knowing the signs and checking in."

Male Digital Founder

"I see the signs early on now. I think – I need a spa, I need to chill out, I need to get over where I have been, I just need a day of fun."

Male Managing Director

Noticing the eyes twitching, the lack of energy or any pain, are all red flags to take note of in advance rather than leaving it until you get to the edge. These creative leaders had learnt from experience, by noticing the body and having an acute awareness of the physical changes that might take place by pre-empting the melt-down that might emerge. One leader emphasises that he had trained himself to be acutely aware of any physiological systems in his body, he can detect the changes and make the necessary adjustments to combat this. Wellbeing comes in many shapes and forms, the design of which, needs to fit the individual context and lifestyle. You can use preventative strategies and ways of operating to create a "way of life" to reduce stress in advance. The mind and body ultimately influence the spirit. This type of thinking indicates that being aware and sensitive to the bodily signs and messages helps you to navigate your way through life. The crucial point is that the body talks to you and that noticing the bodies symptoms and what they are telling you, can help you regularly navigate your way, so that you can pre-empt any serious issues arising.

Learning: it is the journey!

Some of the leaders interviewed viewed resilience as part of their journey and associated it to learning. The reflective leader will look back at the situations encountered to learn from those experiences, accepting challenges and circumstances arising as part of life's journey. In the first chapter, the Journeyer is introduced who sees leadership in terms of the journey whereby you keep adding to your experiences.

The journey

The interview data highlights the viewpoints of some of the leaders discussing the concept of the journey.

> "There is also something around the journey that we are all on our journeys. A part of resilience is about seeing this as a journey."
>
> "And on that journey what sort of journey do you have? Now, people who are resilient will tend to have, I propose, wider and greater experiences than people who are not resilient because people who are not resilient will, by definition, restrain themselves, hold themselves back, will not expose themselves."
>
> Male, experienced Creative Digital Executive Coach

> "I think life's a chain of events isn't it? Makes you who you are, influences then what decisions you make and for me, going to [company name]."
>
> "It is not so much the journey that you go through, because everybody in business will go through a different journey, it's how you use that experience and how you draw on that, and how you react to that, because my experience could be much more far reaching than somebody else's."
>
> "It's not whether you've got different experience or better experience, or less than me, it's how you take that ingredient and you go and plug that gap, if that kind of makes sense."
>
> Female Business Manager

Cultivating resilience helps when seen as part of the journey and not the destination. As the interviewee points out everyone has different experiences as part of their journey and as such it may be the depth of the experience that is significant. Therefore, sharing and listening to each other's experience can help on the journey.

Summary

By taking a pro-active approach to resilience it is possible to deal with unexpected events more easily. Leaders have an array of internal and external strategies they can apply in order to be preventative and to immediately put into place to survive. The focus on wellness is part of a mind-body spirit approach which supports and encourages an approach where awareness is placed on observing the signs in advance. This is about learning to have a deep awareness of your own signs and actively acting on them to be preventative before stress takes hold and takes you to the edge. A smart approach to resilience. Additionally, individual resilience involves appreciating your inner internal experience including allowing your knowingness to be part of a balanced strategy. As such, allowing your inner world experience and sensing capabilities to be recognised as a valid part of your makeup. Going within involves discovering your own inner world, being in the moment, sensing the body through meditation and mindfulness techniques. Added to this, past experiences that you have encountered in your life form part of your DNA and will be supportive of your own unique reactions to dealing with tough times. Your mental attitude is part of your ability to bounce back and bounce forward from life's stresses. In this respect, appreciating the power of positivity and finding strategies for regularly checking into your emotions and positively re-winding any negative inbuilt assumptions will be fruitful. Additionally, externally focusing on reaching out to trusted others for meaningful dialogue is important, along with applying an array of preventative therapeutic activities and exercises in advance. Finding the inner creativity and using the inner and outer strategies with their associated health benefits will encourage resilience.

EXERCISE: SELF-EXPLORE

Food for thought

1. How well have you organised your work-life balance?
2. Does stress rise and disappear at certain times of the year? If so, what makes this happen?
3. Do you have a number of trusted friends/colleagues/confidantes that you can turn to for conversation when in need?
4. Can you deeply open-up to a trusted confidante to be open and vulnerable about the challenges you face?
5. What exercise do you do daily and weekly to keep active?
6. What therapeutic activities are you also involved in on a weekly basis?
7. Are you checking in with your own body on a regular basis to observer and listen for the signs that all is not well? Are you willing to act on this?

8. How often do you use your know-how and intuition to make decisions?
9. Can you make changes quickly? Are you adaptable?
10. What is your attitude to failure and why?
11. What practice might you use to keep a positive mindset?
12. Identify the inner and outer strategies for resilience that you will commit too and put into practice in the future.

References

Chopra D & Tanzi R E (2018) *The Healing Self: A Revolutionary New Plan to Supercharge Your Immunity and Stay Well*, Harmony Books, Random House, New York

Folkman & Moskowitz (2000); Fredrickson (2000) Cited in Fredrickson B L & Joiner T (2002) Positive Emotions Trigger Upward Spirals Towards Emotional Wellbeing, *Research Report American Psychological Society*, 13:2, March

Fredrickson B L (2000a) Extracting Meaning from Past Affective Experiences: The Importance of Peaks, Ends, and Specific Emotions, *Cognition and Emotion*, 14:4, 577–606

Fredrickson B L (2000b) Cultivating Positive Emotions to Optimize Health and Well-Being, *Prevention & Treatment*, March 7, 3

Fredrickson B L (2009) *Positivity: Ground-breaking Research to Release Your Inner Optimist and Thrive*, Oneworld, Oxford Press, Oxford

Fredrickson B L & Joiner T (2002) Positive Emotions Trigger Upward Spirals Towards Emotional Wellbeing, *Research Report American Psychological Society, Psychological Science*, 13:2, 172–175

Neenan M (2018) *Developing Resilience: A Cognitive-Behavioural Approach*, Routledge, Oxon

Northouse P G (2007) *Leadership Theory and Practice*. Cited in Olsen Paul E (2014) Namaste: How Yoga Can Inform Leadership, *Education Journal of Leadership Education*, 13:1, 116–125, Winter 2014

Polanyi M (1967) *The Tacit Dimension*, Anchor Books, New York

Seligman M E P (2011) *Flourish: A New Understanding of Happiness and Wellbeing – and How to Achieve Them*, Nicholas Brearley Publishing, London

Sonnenfield J A & Ward A J (2017) *How Great Leaders Rebound After Career Disasters*. Cited in Resilience (2017) *HBR Emotional Intelligence Series*, Harvard Business Review Press, Boston, MA

Young J (2018–2019) *Research Interview Insights from Leadership and Resilience Study*, The Creative Digital Community, North East, UK. Research first published in this volume

11

THE LEADER AS A DIGITAL SAGE

The challenges of our time are fast and furious in nature. Not only do we have the impact of the digital technologies, but we are experiencing unprecedented challenges. The dynamic and turbulent environment includes a blistering pace of change and the growth of digitization that means managing constant change. In this digital arena, one of the biggest decisions that any future leader will make is the moral ethical decision, over the usage and application of future digital technologies. Notably, this will involve taking care to evaluate the impact of the collateral damage that using digital technologies could place on wider society. The futurist focuses on humanity first and takes into consideration social, environmental and eco factors into the decision-making process to help protect Earth's environment. Digitisation and new forms of working is going to be sustained in the future. Work is now transitioning to hybrid and e-working practice as the technologies evolve. These are the challenges of the twenty-first century. The future leader will need to appreciate the need for collaborative practice, agile working, project management and psychological safety as teams work together in

DOI: 10.4324/9780367280970-11

virtual space. The leader will also need to develop their own style of leadership that contributes positively to radiate hope and optimism to staff. By their very nature, this leader will apply preventative strategies that support personal resilience for all concerned so that they can be supported in turbulent times.

Strategies for personal resilience

Individual resilience is having an awareness of both the internal and external experiences. It is about appreciating, applying and developing an array of internal and external strategies as part of an armour of tactics for survival in an increasingly unpredictable world. Ultimately, it is about taking a responsible and proactive holistic approach to personal resilience, inclusive of mind, body and spirit for wellbeing. Hence, choosing your plan for resilience involves using a selection of multiple strategies on a regular basis.

Developing internal strategies for personal resilience

The past experiences that we have encountered in life form part our personal DNA and will be supportive of our own unique reactions to dealing with tough times. These past experiences may have created in-built assumptions and mental attitudes that support the ability to bounce back (or bounce forward), or not, from adversity. In this respect, developing an appreciation for the power of positivity and finding strategies to reframe and re-wind the inbuilt assumptions, will be fruitful. In the mix of inner resilience are self-awareness and the alignment to personal and professional values, in order to become your authentic self in all situations. Therefore, going within and exploring self may involve discovering your own inner world, being in the moment, sensing the body and applying meditation and mindfulness techniques to encounter the health benefits that may arise. The internal aspect involves the ability to sense our own body and appreciate that body talks to you. In this way, you are tracking the subtle conversation your body is having with you before a flare up. This means being on the alert by reading the signs and signals. The voice from the research data highlighted that it was necessary to follow your energy as your energy levels will tell you when you are in the flow and when you are drained. As such, being switched on to your energy (or spirit), enables you to identify and build on what brings you positivity and as a result happiness. Additionally, personal resilience may involve acknowledging your internal knowingness, hunches, intuition and gut feel to help make crucial decisions. Consequently, this allows your inner knowingness and sensing capabilities to become a recognised and valid part of your makeup.

Developing external strategies for personal resilience

Personal resilience is also about applying external interactions including the powerful tactics of reaching out to trusted others, in the form of confidants, friends, family and professional contacts. This means connecting through conversation and dialogue and exploring and sharing mental models and assumptions stored in our mind. In this way, reaching out to those you

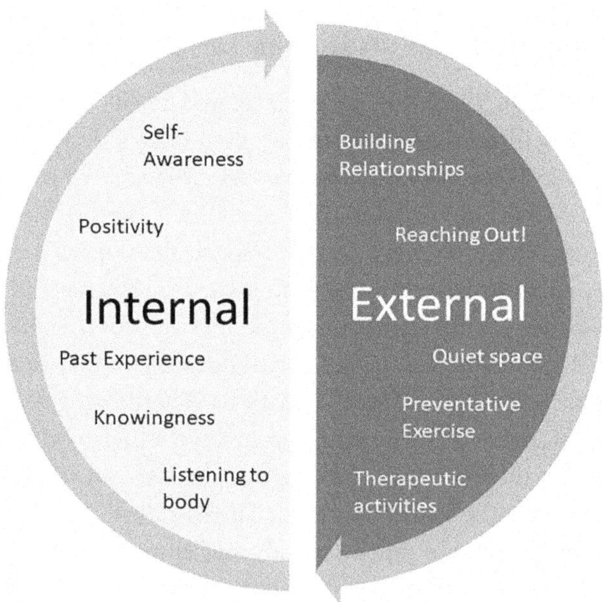

Figure 11.1 Internal and external personal resilience for leaders

Source: Young (2018–2019)

deeply trust involves your ability to be vulnerable and to engage in deep meaningful authentic conversations. Relationship integrity, trust and authenticity are therefore key to reaching out. External strategies are an added layer of pre-planned preventative activities that help the body survive and enable you to de-stress regularly to cope with adversity. This involves being preventative by being pro-active through doing daily and weekly physical exercises and activity, focusing on wellness practices and relaxing therapeutic activity. Figure 11.1 highlights the internal and external activities. All these activities are ways to de-stress and maintain a good work-life balance. Finding creative time and space to de-stress regularly enables you to tap into your creativity.

The leader as a Digital Sage

What do future leaders need to do to survive in a future where there is a state of continuous change? The old static order has been replaced by a transient state of flux where the traditional management principles no longer apply. Leaders need to be able to think outside the box and develop their creativity. Creativity, innovation and experimentation are important components for future survival and leaders need to be digital savvy explorers applying creative, agile, flexible design techniques. Additionally, they need to develop their collaborative capacity, embrace failure and critique, and focus on developing a supportive, open, creative, safe culture to create synergy and build transformation. In a digital era, this leader needs to have a strong moral/ethical compass. This leader is a Digital Sage.

The DNA for a Digital Sage is presented next. The Sage leads in the digital era through authenticity, collaboration, self-awareness, self-reflection and continuous learning. By doing so, the Sage is confident of their own abilities. The Digital Sage aligns personal values to the values of the organisation (professional values), so that there is a match between who they are and what they represent. As an authentic leader they are open and transparent to those around them. They use emotional intelligence and empathy to stand in the shoes of others in order to interact with colleagues. The Sage is a digital savvy futurist who keeps up to date on the impact of technology and consequently creates new strategies for the business in the ever-moving volatile environment that they find themselves in. The Digital Sage is not only a strategist but a first-hand communicator. The Sage is a golfer who knows how to use the right style of leadership within the right context; however, the overarching style is to be authentic and pursue a coaching style to develop staff. The Sage is also customer-centric and as is appropriate in the contemporary fast-moving environment focuses and acts on feedback from customers and stakeholders. The added qualities of a Sage are that they use their powers of diplomacy making best use of conversation and dialogue to solve problems. Moreover, the Sage cares about the wellbeing of those around them and works in a quiet, settled manner honouring and applying a moral ethical compass. As an ethical leader, the Digital Sage keeps an eye on future developments and makes decisions based on the greater good for both business and society. The Sage is up to date, digital savvy, innovate and creative. The future leader in modern society needs to develop into a Digital Sage and be viewed as a Journeyer who is comfortable with failure because they know it helps them to learn and unlearn on their journey. See the Digital Sage outlined in Figure 11.2.

The Components of the Digital Sage

New Framework: the Features of the Digital Sage

The future leader in the twenty-first century shows the eight distinctive facets of a Digital Sage including: Journeyer, Yogi, Digital Strategist, Situational Golfer, Connector and Relationship Builder, Positive Psychologist, Ethical Ambassador and Creative Explorer. No one facet dominates and all elements contribute to the making of a Digital Sage. The notion of a model/framework for a Digital Sage has arisen from the literature reviewed and from the voice of the leaders from the research interviews conducted in this study. The Sage oozes wisdom, calmness, energy, reflection and resilience. The facets of the Digital Sage are discussed next.

Journeyer

The Journeyer appreciates that it is the journey and not the destination that counts and implements the principle of fast failure in the context of the blistering pace of change. The Journeyer focuses upon lessons learnt from experience and is deeply reflective. The Journeyer lives reflective practice as part of management development and understands that change is a constantly lived experience. The Journeyer is curious and encourages others to be curious. They are comfortable with ambiguity and appreciate that effective

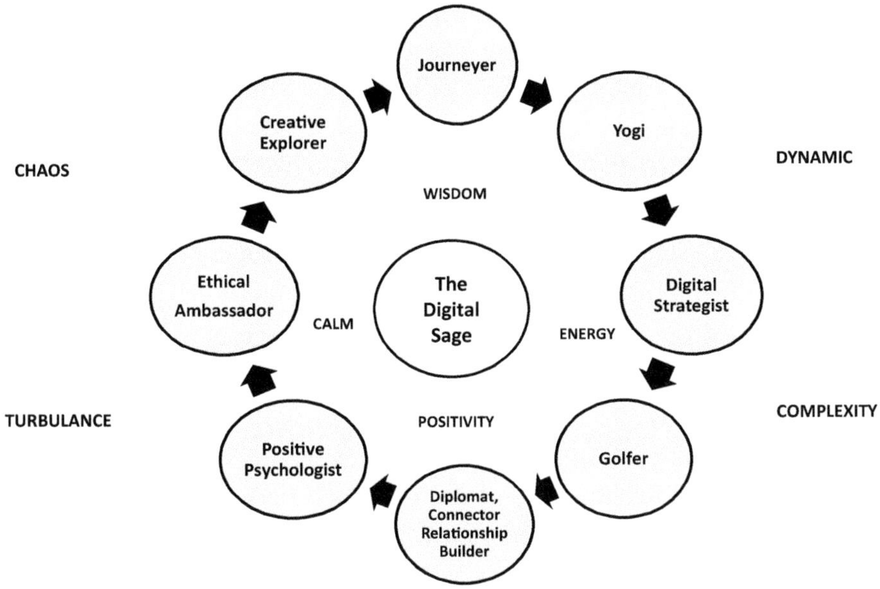

Figure 11.2 The leader as a Digital Sage

Source: Young (2018–2019)

learning is not linear. The Journeyer is the apprentice, nomad, trekker and navigator and places value on the experiences encountered along the journey.

Yogi

The yogi draws upon his/her deep inner strength in a quiet way. Ultimately, the yogi is self-aware and continues to develop personal self-awareness whilst developing empathy for others. The yogi is authentic, supple and at ease with him/herself. Yogis understand "being in the present" and quietly go about their business. The yogi not only understands self but by diving deeply within reaches deep levels of resilience. A yogi leader knows that to find answers they must go within themselves and retreat to a quiet space to practice mindfulness, meditation and breathing techniques to support wellbeing. For the yogi, exercise is vital for good health and they make time out for exercise, walking and therapeutic activity to help revitalises the body and create energy. The yogi is intrinsically appreciative of diversity. Yogis are essentially authentic leaders showing openness and honesty in all aspects of leadership. Wellness is the yogi heartland, and all aspects of wellness are part of their DNA. The yogi leads from the front in a quiet and calm manner, creating psychological safety for those around them. The yogi keeps calm whilst change swirls around them as they use a range of tactics to find creative outlets and enter into quiet space for contemplation of the issues at hand.

Digital Strategist

The digital leader operates within an increasingly digital world and has acquired the ability to successfully navigate this terrain. This digital category of leader creates visibility and vision, operating within both the hybrid virtual and physical workspace and is tech savvy. The strategist will have a vision for the future and be able to operate from a helicopter position hovering above by using a big picture approach to gather perspective. The strategist actively seeks to keep up to date with macro trends and new developments on the horizon that might impact the business. The strategist creates the blueprint for the future and plans and executes the roadmap, whilst at the same time being open to acting upon feedback on the unforeseen changes appearing on the skyline. In the digital era they scan for new opportunities and are alert to the impact of new digital technology that could potentially transform the business. The digital leader uses their antenna to show a strategic awareness of the possibilities that may emerge in a very dynamic fast-paced future environment and as such readily embrace change and adjust and transform through business model innovation. The digital leader understands the impact of digital transformation upon the business model and, as such, fully expect change. Such a leader is customer-centric and understands the winds of change in both physical and digital environments where the customer is part of a dis-abandoning economy, and in this case the connector needs to be sensitive and agile to online customer needs. Additionally, they appreciate and explore the potential for stimulating innovation and entrepreneurship.

Golfer

The golf player identifies "plug and play" styles of leadership that they will apply according to task, context and situation. These styles may comprise of visionary; coach; democrat; affiliate; pacesetter and commander, as discussed in Chapter 6. They appreciate that two of these styles are detractors and not appealing (commander and pacesetter) and that four are positive attractors (visionary, coach, democrat and affiliate). The commanding leadership position may come into play on the occasion of a serious emergency only where the leader has no option but to step up (plug and play) to handle the situation that has occurred in this emergency. A variety of these styles are used when appropriate, in relation to the assessed situation, and the leader develops and shapes their understanding of the context they find themselves in. Fundamentally, situational leadership is crucial to understand but other styles of leadership add to this. Additionally, the twenty-first century digital leader is an authentic leadership, and this practice needs to be developed, along with a coaching style for digital teamwork.

Connector and Relationship Builder

Conversation and dialogue are powerful communication tools we use to connect with other humans. A conversation helps you clarify your own thoughts by testing them out on others and modifying them while moving forward. Sharing of mental models, concepts and ideas is part of this process. This leader understands the power of communication, builds networks and uses dialogue and conversation to resolve issues, persuade and reflect. More importantly, these leaders build a network of trustful relationships with experts in the field by creating genuine sustainable long-term relationships. They will reach out to trusted others in their network in times of need, as part of their strategy for personal resilience. The relationship builder is an authentic communicator who applies empathy as part of his tool set. This communicator has high levels of advanced communication skills and develops the diplomatic skills required for virtual interactions. The adaptable digital leader focuses on creating and building trustful relationships on both a personal and professional level. They enable, empower and appreciate the diverse perspectives of the team. In this way building a strong and genuine network to reach out to in times of need to support ongoing resilience. The digital strategist understands intangible value of this network of relationships, and connections.

Positive Psychologist

The Positive Psychologist shows awareness of the power of positive emotions. They build up their own psychological capital – a bank of positivity. Creating positive currency can decrease anxiety, reduce symptoms of illness and improve the quality of your sleep. This is part of building resilience with a positive cognitive intervention. Wellbeing takes the stage front and centre, and happiness (or positive emotion) becomes one of the five pillars of positive psychology, along with positive relations, engagement, meaningfulness and positive accomplishment. A positive mind-set offers an array of positivity and flow that enables the individual to flourish. An awareness of the impact that positive psychology can play in your everyday life helps in all situations. The Digital Sage applies positive psychology and appreciates how it works on self and other staff to build on energy and wellbeing whilst staying in the flow.

Ethical Ambassador

A moral/ethical compass is required for decision-making processes in the digital tech era. Throughout the book the focus has been upon ethical decisions in relation to using the new technologies that are emerging. What needs to be considered is the impact and consequences that a decision might have upon future society in the long term. Commonly known as collateral damage. In the technically advanced and environmentally conscious digital era, developing as an ethical ambassador is imperative for a future created for the greater good of individuals and society. Not only is the ambassador ethical but is authentic and lives in alignment with their true self.

Creative Explorer

The Creative Explorer appreciates that experiments are necessary – that we need to think outside the box to survive and be enterprising. A creative leader appreciates fast failure and feedback and creates a culture of psychological safety to support learning and experimentation. The Creative Explorer finds a quiet place in which to retreat, spend time and nourish self when necessary. They know the benefits of allowing themselves quiet time in a frenetic fast-moving environment. Quieting the mind means less thinking, calculating, judging, worrying, fearing, hoping, trying, regretting, controlling or distracting in order to be in the moment and let go of self-judgement. Like the yogi, the Creative Explorer uses mindfulness and meditation techniques to quiet the mind and return to the moment. The creative understands the power of listening to the inner world. They listen to the body and read the cues and signs and act on them, appreciating that the body talks to you. These leaders establish what brings them energy and follow the flow to be at ease and in alignment with themselves. In this way, reconnecting with their true self and letting go of the false (faux) self that may have been created. The creative may also use music and humour as part of their arsenal. They encourage innovation through experimentation, iterative techniques and agile thinking and are comfortable with non-finished versions. The Creative Explorer is open minded, willing to let go and experiment and are happy to explore new creative ideas.

Summary

The contemporary leader appreciates the need to assemble personal strategies for resilience for themselves and those around them. This includes an array of inner and outer strategies that create a multi-faceted, integral holistic approach to personal resilience that encompasses mind, body and spirit. Additionally, the facets previously discussed represent a Digital Sage who uses these components to lead in a resilient manner. This leader is an ethical leader who has the ability and strength to hold their own, who lead by example, and work towards the greater good. The Sage manages the change, builds a psychologically safe culture in the workplace, establishes meaningful and trustworthy relationships and connects and reaches out to trusted others when in need. The Sage appreciates that leaders are required to recognise the elements of good leadership and develop their own style whilst creating an organisation for an unknowable future. The Digital Sage as a leader intrinsically stays calm, is self-aware, authentic, respectful, emotionally intelligent, empathetic, creative, adaptive, reflective, and a fun learner and Journeyer. In particular, the Sage will develop self-awareness and align to their personal and professional values to invoke and live their authentic nature. They use internal elements of resilience by tapping into their own unique past experiences that made them who they are. This leader appreciates the need to take time out to listen to the body; exercise; use therapeutic relaxation techniques; focus on the positive psychology of the mind; and listen to their own inner knowing. The Digital Sage stays calm in turbulent times and in so doing acts as a shelter to those around until the storm passes.

Reference

Young J (2018–2019) *Research Interview Insights on Resilience Study*, The Creative Digital Community, North East, UK. Research first published in this volume

INDEX

For Product Safety Concerns and Information please contact our EU representative GPSR@taylorandfrancis.com
Taylor & Francis Verlag GmbH, Kaufingerstraße 24, 80331 München, Germany

www.ingramcontent.com/pod-product-compliance
Ingram Content Group UK Ltd.
Pitfield, Milton Keynes, MK11 3LW, UK
UKHW022019180926
475701UK00005B/922

* 9 7 8 1 0 3 2 0 4 7 7 4 4 *